# THE CONSERVATIVE REVOLUTION

# THE
# CONSERVATIVE
# REVOLUTION

Cory Bernardi

**Connor Court Publishing**
**Ballarat**

Published in 2013 by Connor Court Publishing Pty Ltd

PO Box 224W
Ballarat VIC 3350
sales@connorcourt.com
www.connorcourt.com

ISBN: 9781922168962 (pbk.)

Cover design by Ian James

Printed in Australia

# CONTENTS

# About the Author

**Cory Bernardi** has been a Senator for South Australia in the Australian Parliament since 2006.

Before entering parliament he was a member of the Australian rowing team, a publican, an investment portfolio manager and a venture capital entrepreneur. He has also served on the board of the Australian Sports Commission and as Chairman of the Australian Sports Foundation.

He has had over 25 years' involvement in the Liberal Party, becoming the youngest ever State President of the Liberal Party in South Australia and the youngest ever Federal Vice President of the Liberal Party of Australia.

Cory has presented and spoken on five continents about politics, leadership, motivation, business and investment. His previous publications include two books for children: *The Money Tree* and *Fit for Life!* and four collections of his regular columns, *As I See It, No Left Turn, On The Right Track* and *Outside The Beltway*. Cory is committed to fostering conservative thought and values. In 2009 he founded the Conservative Leadership Foundation – a not-for-profit educational, research and training organisation dedicated to developing Australia's future leaders.

He lives in Adelaide with his wife Sinead and their two sons.

His personal website can be found at *www.corybernardi.com*

# Preface

## A few words about language

Before we begin, I believe it is necessary to clarify some key terms and language the reader will encounter in the pages that follow.

I will use the term *radical* and *radicals* because I believe that the ideas promoted by these people are fundamentally at odds with natural law, the traditions and cultural wealth that we have inherited from our forefathers, and are therefore diametrically in opposition to what is best for society and the individual. For these reasons their proposed policy changes are 'radical' by definition. I will also use terms such as *'progressive'* in scare quotes because I believe that their ideas are the opposite of progress, and in fact lead to social dissolution, poverty and a sense of loss. The use of 'progressive' as a name for their political agenda and as a title for the people who advocate radical reforms is a misnomer; I cannot dignify it by legitimising their use of this word without qualification. Although I understand that the left-right dichotomy may have increasingly little relevance in political debate today, it is a useful point of reference when discussing policy in theoretical terms. Therefore, *left* and *leftist* will be used to make general reference to those political and social forces that are opposed to the traditional principles outlined throughout this volume.

It is important to note that I will also use words such as *freedom*, *liberty*, *choice* and the like throughout this small book. Unfortunately, these words have largely been hijacked by the left in its agenda of false 'liberation' against tradition and those things that the conservative will hold dear. The words have also been abused by certain self-professing conservatives whose ideas about conservative theory are essentially materialist and economist. Some have even appealed to these words to undermine traditional conservative position on social policy. Where possible, I will try to qualify and explain what I mean by the use of these words as I use them.

Sometimes, when the terms are used for the sake of convenience, I ask only that the reader considers the substance of my work, which is where the message naturally lies. This volume is not, however, intended to be a comprehensive dissertation on conservative theory; it should of course be read along with other books which will provide further depth and insight to the interested or curious reader. Many of the concepts that are referred to here have already been discussed and analysed elsewhere by other writers, theorists, philosophers and thinkers of our conservative tradition.

## Who and what is this volume about?

There are three types of people in Australian political life. These are the three broad groups around which the future of policy is determined and by whom the future direction of Australia is shaped and determined.

The first of these are the **radicals** who are constantly trying to tear down our institutions and diminish our historical values because these don't fit with their own view of how the world should function.

The second group, by far the largest, is characteristic of those who typically strive for a better life for themselves and their families, free of political or other interference. These people are consumed with the daily routines of life: earning a living, raising a family, and generally being productive members of their local communities. They rarely have time for political activism because the routines of life will undoubtedly devour most if not all of their time, energy and resources. Unlike the first group, these people are rarely heard, other than on election day. For this reason, they are frequently referred to as the '**Silent Majority**'. As a consequence, they may appear to be apathetic to the societal changes going on around them, but only until it affects them and their families personally. They are the ones targeted by radicals and conservatives alike, but that is only because this group is the most important of the three: they are the ones who ultimately determine the fate of society.

The third are the **conservatives** who seek to protect and defend the structures and values that have allowed our nation to achieve the traditional freedoms and prosperity that we enjoy today.

This brief volume explores the timeless principles from which some of those structures and values derive, and how they can be applied to social and economic policy. It attempts to explain why they should be supported and the consequences should they be neglected or rejected outright. It looks to explain why the conservative is the natural representative of the aspirations of the majority, and it seeks to empower and equip the conservative with arguments to defeat the corrosive negativity of radicals and leftists.

In short, the values and structures the conservative seeks to protect are based on principles that are under threat from the dominant ideologies of social reform by the left and the increasingly secular and opportunistic society which creates a fertile ground for their ideas to grow. A society in which concepts of right and wrong have been replaced with a moral relativism is a society where there are no absolutes – only preferences or choices. It is a society where there is an excuse for everything and responsibility for nothing; a society where the wisdom of the ages is being replaced by momentary fads and quick fixes.

That is why we need a conservative revolution; a revolution that will restore conservative values to their rightful place as the guiding principles of our civilisation and the cornerstone of governance. We need a revolution that will see Australia return to the traditions that have sustained it since federation; the same traditions that have allowed all free nations to flourish.

Only through returning to these conservative principles can our nation confront the challenges that face us and work toward a confident and sovereign Australia, a country which has the will and strength necessary to prosper in an increasingly globalising and often hostile world.

The essays which follow seek to examine various facets of Australian life and applies conservative principles to demonstrate their practical and existential benefits to society. This is not intended to be an exhaustive examination of all the issues or to provide comprehensive solutions, but it seeks to highlight the key areas and their importance to our future. Society is a complex creature, and the conservative is not interested in creating blueprints for all aspects of governance, human activity and commerce, because the conservative knows that this is simply impossible. What the conservative does do, however, is acknowledge the essential ingredients necessary for an ordered, safe and prosperous society to exist, and these are often expressed in the ideas that conservatives hold dear. Through these ideals we can forge a brighter and more promising future for Australia. It is my hope that this volume will make a modest contribution to that future. The elusive 'good' that leftists continue to seek through legislative and policy reform is nowhere to be seen. Since the social revolution of the 1960s, we have seen so-called 'progressive' reforms causing more trouble and problems than they could have ever hoped to solve. It is time to reclaim conservatism as the philosophy for individual liberty and human happiness.

# 1

# A Time for Choosing

I have never considered myself a revolutionary. Revolution has always been seen as the preserve of the political left whose commitment to change is led by a loathing of the *status quo*, rootlessness and the desire to seek change for change's sake.

Even the term 'revolutionary' and its noun 'revolution' are inextricably linked in the minds of most of us with leftist guerrillas like Ernesto 'Che' Guevara: an apparently charismatic mass murderer and leading figure of the Cuban revolution, whose image has ironically become a pop-cultural fashion statement, a sales and marketing exercise for capitalist T-shirt manufacturers.

But it *is* time for a revolution in this country: a revolution that will restore the principles and values that have successfully guided mankind and our society since the dawn of time.

We need to restore that which is now routinely ignored in the blind pursuit of new agendas that are remarkable not for their lack of substance, but because they are built on the economic and moral corpses of previous failure.

We need to reacquaint our citizens with the understanding that there are absolute truths that hold true in all places and at all times.

We need to make a radical departure from the growing and all-pervasive acceptance that critical and discerning moral judgment is somehow unfair and an infringement on human rights.

We need to re-establish the notion that taking responsibility for consequences is just as important as freedom of choice.

We need to reaffirm that the family is the most important building block in any society and that the wellbeing of children is the best investment that any society can make.

We need to recognise that our nation has a role to play in international affairs but her primary responsibility is to her citizens.

In short, we need not just any revolution, we need a *conservative* revolution.[1] One that will re-establish the family, the social and economic virtues that have been neglected for at least two generations, yet are as innate within the human spirit today as they ever have been.

## Australia today:
### *Constitution, complacency and crisis*

In many respects, Australia today is the envy of the world. We are blessed with a nation that is pluralistic and dynamic: it is abundant with natural resources, has a strong food production capacity, a largely pristine environment and a welcoming citizenry. We are a nation established on a commitment to supporting the values of personal initiative, reward for effort and a 'fair go' for all. Our inherited political traditions have established one of the oldest and most stable democracies in the world, conceived by wise forebears who adopted the Westminster parliamentary system from Great Britain and combined it with the federal model of the United States. This has resulted in a unique and enduring Australian Constitution which has remarkably survived the political turbulence of the 20th century: two

---

1 Or as the traditionalist philosopher Plinio Corrêa de Oliviera states, a 'counter-revolution': *Revolution and Counter-Revolution* (Tradition Family Property, 3rd ed. 1993) p. 60.

World Wars, the Great Depression, the Cold War and a constitutional crisis in 1975.

Our Constitution provides a roadmap for our system of government. It wisely divides the responsibilities of government between the states and Commonwealth to ensure that the concentration of power remains elusive from those that may wish to use it to curtail civil liberties.

Of course, many will argue that the fear of a concentration of government power in this modern age is an irrational one. They may be right, but we are wiser to trust in the separation of powers to protect our freedom and interests, than in the transient nature of political promises and ideology.

Indeed, one of the greatest dangers confronting us is complacency or intemperance. We must resist the temptation to believe that our course is set and cannot be altered, that what has been always will be and that government is the answer to every problem. We must also avoid committing to feel-good knee-jerk policy initiatives that seem good today but into which little thought has been put. Prudence and a careful analysis of perceived problems is preferable to thoughtless reaction.

The Global Financial Crisis (GFC) of 2008 illustrated how quickly the political pendulum can swing. Amid a chorus heralding the 'death of capitalism' and the need for a common global regulatory framework, we witnessed the nationalisation of industry and banking on a scale unprecedented since the First World War, or perhaps even outside of the Communist Bloc countries themselves. Alarmingly, though such radical action was done under the guise of helping the global economic recovery, few questioned the long-term cost of such policies, both economic and social.

In seeking to improve their circumstance, many Western governments grasped at the failed centralist policies of the political left, whilst refusing to acknowledge the core issues that led them down the path towards the parlous economic circumstance they were suffering.

While the left will regard the cause of the GFC as the lack of government intervention in the free market, the reality is somewhat different. Indeed, many of the problems that caused the GFC can actually be *attributed* to government intervention. In the United States this included policies that mandated home loans for the unemployed, financial bailouts for failed businesses and a culture that sought to prop up consumer consumption at almost any cost. Like much of American culture, these philosophies spread throughout the Western world with similar and catastrophic results: asset price bubbles, massive consumer debt and huge consumption spending were to inevitably follow.

When it became apparent that consumers could not continue to borrow money and spend their way to seemingly unlimited prosperity, the government stepped in to try to alleviate the pain. The relaxation of interest rates to record lows further fuelled the resulting 'bubble economy' and encouraged further borrowing and risk taking. The ultimate result was the global financial meltdown of 2008.

Despite the obvious contribution of government to the GFC, the anti-conservative movements sought to use the situation as an excuse to further deconstruct capitalism and Western culture with talk of a 'new beginning'. This involved increasing the size and influence of government, establishing international agreements that would bind sovereign nations to the direction of unelected bodies and a philosophical repudiation of capitalism.

This increased concentration of power in the hands of the state is rejected by the conservative as a threat to individual liberty. The GFC, the policies that lead to it and the misguided responses which followed, are but one example of the intemperate and thoughtless reaction by governments of the broader-left. The resulting centralisation of executive authority and the growth of power among non-representative bodies is deeply concerning to the conservative voter, policy analyst and politician. These issues will be further elaborated later in this volume.

## Room for improvement:
### *The renovation of a nation*

While rejecting the growth of statist organisations, there is no doubt that there is room for improvement in Australian society today. Appropriate reform, when necessary, is not inimical to conservative thought. Society can be a complex creature, and being organic, it can also be unpredictable in its evolution over time. Changing conditions, both global and local, cannot be avoided or ignored; they must be addressed and dealt with appropriately. This is acknowledged by governments and individuals in their changes to policy settings through which they seek to strengthen the nation and improve its prospects of growing into a regional leader, one which our neighbours can hold up as a model society worthy of respect and imitation.

However, for all the advances in technology, science and communications, there are signs that we are failing in areas where it matters most: *our personal relationships and society in general.* The atomisation of society evidenced by the startling increase in recent decades of single person households[2] and the identification of

---

2 Australian Bureau of Statistics 2012, *2012 Year Book Australia*, cat. No. 1301.0, ABS, Canberra, p. 264.

loneliness and isolation as one of our most pressing new social problems, should give us cause for concern.

To ignore the importance of the social compact between individuals and communities, in favour of a top-down, government-driven ideology, is to pursue a dangerous path.

We need to learn to ask the hard question: is this vortex unavoidable or can we do something about it? Do we allow our society to be demolished (with no real confidence about what might replace it) or do we have the courage to renovate? These will undoubtedly be the questions on the forefront of conservative thought as we approach the challenges of the 21st century.

## Returning to enduring values and principles

That is why we need a conservative revolution; a revolution based not on the removal of government, but the restoration of values and principles that guide good government in its work; a revolution for a type of society that we seek for ourselves and for the generations to come, one which creates a new franchise with the majority, empowering a disengaged citizenry, taking the power to determine their destiny from bureaucrats and returning it back into the hands of the individual.

Only by returning to conservative principles can our nation confidently confront the challenges that face us, endure times of hardship and prosperity with equanimity, and work towards an Australia which is dynamic, confident, and growing in international stature.

However, before one can advocate for a philosophically conservative framework to be restored as the cornerstone of our national governance, one should at least attempt to define what it means to be a conservative. This presents the first difficulty, for there is no one conservative doctrine or ideology.

To complicate matters further, many conservative thinkers have argued that conservatism is not (or should not be) a doctrine or ideology at all. Michael Oakeshott wrote that conservatism "is not a creed or a doctrine, but a disposition."[3] Likewise, the late Kenneth Minogue suggests that ideology is the natural 'trade' of "the pedagogic, the communicative, and the administrative classes" who are isolated and therefore 'detached' from the 'direct' experience of routine life.[4] This reinforces the view that 'progressive' politics is based on abstract concepts and contrasts this with the grounded, practical orientation of conservative thought. Conservatism, therefore, is a way of life; in the words of US conservative thinker Peter Viereck, it is a sentiment where the "fruitful nostalgia for the permanent beneath the flux" guides reform.[5] Another theorist, John Kekes, writes that "the source of conservatism is a natural attitude that combines the enjoyment of something valued with the fear of losing it" and that:

> Natural conservatism values and aims to protect the tried and true; both together, because the tried alone may have little in its favor and much against it and because the true needs to be tried, and tried again, to be shown to be indeed true.[6]

Yet others, such as Roger Scruton, have found that articulating a 'doctrine' is necessary to "outline a system of belief" to counter modern theoretical leftism. "The reality of politics is action" writes

---

3 Michael Oakeshott, *Rationalism in Politics* (Basic Books, 1962) p. 168.
4 Kenneth Minogue, *The Servile Mind – How Democracy Erodes the Moral Life* (Encounter Books, 2010) p. 207.
5 Peter Viereck, *Conservatism Revisited* (Transaction, 2009; originally Charles Scribner's Sons, 1949) p. 70. This was the first post-War book published in the United States with the term 'conservative' in its title. Viereck remains largely unknown, but his contribution to post-War traditionalist thought has not been insignificant.
6 John Kekes, *A Case for Conservatism* (Cornell University, 1998) p. 5.

Scruton, "but action derives, however covertly, from thought, and consistent action demands consistent thought."[7] It is this 'consistent thought' that we must define if we wish to confront the modern left with a robust system of ideas and policies for cultural restoration.

Of course, conservatism is a body of opinion that has been professed and developed by prominent writers and public advocates for over two centuries. It is built on principles established far earlier than that; but the great works of Anglo-Australian conservatism (indeed the conservative traditions of all British derived political systems) began with Edmund Burke in his *Reflections on the Revolution in France* (1790).

In Burke's writing, we see that conservatism is a state of mind that reflects and honours the importance of stability and structure. This attitude has been reflected in later conservative thinkers across the Anglosphere, as illustrated briefly above. It recognises that the historic continuity of human experience offers a better guide to policy than the abstract, utopian propositions of those who seek to reinvent the human condition in their own image (or that of Rousseau, J.S. Mill, Marx, Freud and their acolytes). Yet conservatives know that "prudent change is the means of our preservation, and the great statesman is one who combines with a disposition to preserve an ability to improve."[8]

Indeed, there is no model conservative due to the inherently variable nature of the human condition and the particular traditions that it creates. This will naturally result in a wide and greatly varied multiplicity of different communities, social systems and structures

---

7 Roger Scruton, *The Meaning of Conservatism* (3rd ed., St Augustine's Press, 2002; originally Palgrave, 1980) p. 1.
8 Russel Kirk, address to the Heritage Foundation at the University Club, Washington D.C., United States of America (4 June 1980).

across the globe. Conservatism reflects the character of an individual and his rejection of any particular abstract ideology. This is because it is sustained by fluid sentiments rather than rigid dogmata. This is reflected in the accommodation of the diverse views on any number of subjects by those who identify themselves as conservative. There is perhaps no better proof of this than the fact that many of these conservatives will frequently argue among each other, almost as often as they do against the left, and sometimes with great passion and vitriol.

Russell Kirk suggested that it is not possible to outline a concise catalogue of conservative convictions. However, he did offer general principles, to which most conservatives would subscribe, even if some may stress the greater importance or significance of one or another.[9]

I offer my interpretation of Kirk's original principles below. It should be noted that since the publication of his opus, many of them have undergone various stages of development and interpretation. What follows is my own understanding of their meaning, particularly in the context of an Australian conservatism. Where I believe it is necessary, I have made slight digressions to develop a point which will be important to bear in mind while working through the chapters that follow. I acknowledge that my observations are based closely on his original work and should not be considered original thought.

## 1. *An enduring moral order*

Order and stability are at the very cornerstone of functional society. Without order there is chaos, and chaos is not a state conducive to human achievement and happiness. Indeed, without order and stability one could argue there is no society as such because society requires

---

9 'A Conservatism of Thought and Imagination', The Russell Kirk Center for Cultural Renewal, Michigan, United States of America (undated) <www.kirkcenter.org> (accessed 26 July 2013).

some form of consensus as to the moral and legal framework within which people live and interact with each other.

However, conservatives question what limits should be placed on achieving order. Coercive force, for example, would be anathema to most conservative thought and policy. It is more often a product of leftist initiatives that lead to tyrannical government which subverts the individual conscience with a collective dogma. Far better for order to be achieved, not at the barrel of a gun, but as a product of an enduring moral code innate to every individual and which percolates naturally through the structures of society. When men and women are internally governed by a clear sense of right and wrong, government coercion is simply not necessary and society will naturally flourish and prosper.

Whatever political system a given society inherits, it will always do better where citizens have a belief in justice, honour and private morality. Where individuals are reduced to the satisfaction of personal appetites society will decline. The need to preserve society is at the very heart of conservatism and the absolute moral truths that are required for this preservation are not subject to change.

This is why *we need a conservative revolution*.

## 2. *Custom, convention and continuity*

Custom and convention are an intrinsic part of our law and they enable us to live together peaceably – what we sometimes call 'tradition'. They are enduring systems that have been passed through the ages, allowing successive generations to maintain a linkage with the past, and to preserve hard won moral capital: what G.K. Chesterton called "the democracy of the dead".[10]

While appreciating that past practice is not always appropriate to changing times, it is the knowledge accumulated over generations of

---

10 Gilbert Keith Chesterton, *Orthodoxy* (Hendrickson, 2006; originally 1908) p. 43.

fruitful living, the consequences of persistent customs which form our particular traditions over time, the wealth and wisdom that these represent, that is attractive to the conservative mind. The conservative is therefore not against change itself. This can be traced to the legacy of Edmund Burke, who advised that conservatives welcomed *prudent* change as a means of building on the achievements of our forebears.[11]

Essentially, the conservative rejects the radical overthrow of the institutions and interests that have guided society through the centuries and cautions that necessary change should be gradual and discriminatory.

This is why *we need a conservative revolution.*

### 3. *Principle of prescription*

The conservative accepts that we are able to see further than our ancestors because we stand on their shoulders, having learned from their mistakes and their successes.

While welcoming the discoveries and advances made in the modern era, the conservative also accepts that the very core of human nature and the moral code through which mankind is internally governed is fundamentally immutable.

Thus the acceptance of the principle of prescription, which Kirk describes as "things established by immemorial usage,"[12] is a key part of allowing society to progress and develop in a sustainable manner.

Unfortunately, it seems that most politicians and policy analysts

---

11 For a discussion of Burke's concept of prudence and related concepts, see Joseph Baldacchino, 'The Value-Centred Historicism of Edmund Burke', *Modern Age,* vol. 27, no. 2 (Spring 1983) specifically at p. 142. Baldacchino's dissertation was recently reproduced in *Humanitas* (online) (National Humanities Institute, 27 March 2012) <www.nhinet.org> (accessed 11 July 2013), see op cit at ¶ 20.

12 Russel Kirk, Heritage Foundation Lecture, Washington D.C., United States of America (20 March 1986).

today treat anything that claims to be 'progress' as a desirable thing irrespective of where its ideas may have come from and where they may lead; this means that anything that is correspondingly juxtaposed as 'old' is devalued. This narrow-minded approach to national development is another reason why *we need a conservative revolution.*

### 4. *Principle of prudence*

Plato claimed that prudence was chief among the virtues. Burke, as the father of modern conservatism, agreed. Decisions should be judged by their long-term consequences, not short-term results or the momentary and necessarily fleeting popularity among a restless and intemperate populace.

Imprudent action, so often advocated by radical reformists, often results in the curative change being far worse than the ills that preceded it.[13] The conservative believes that action should only be taken after sufficient reflection and assessment of the consequences to future generations, rather than the immediate benefits to the present one.

This kind of thinking is lacking among our political class and this is why *we need a conservative revolution.*

### 5. *Principle of variety*

The preservation of society requires healthy diversity, but not in the subversive sense in which the word is often (and mischievously) used by radicals, 'progressives' and other leftists. The quest to remove all inequality is the deadening hand of socialism and results in social stagnation. Where there is true variety, there will be inevitable 'inequality' – that is simply the result of human nature and the pluralism that defines us as a people. In striving to remove all forms

---

13 This important defining quality of conservative thought, which can be described as simply a cautious scepticism, is elaborated in detail in Roger Scruton, *The Uses of Pessimism and the Danger of False Hope* (Atlantic Books, 2010).

of natural and institutional differences in pursuit of a utopian society (outside of the rule of natural law), the radical wrecker allows one form of inequity to be replaced by another.

Given the same opportunities, any two people will not achieve the same results due to their inherently different qualities, talents, capabilities and desires. This is celebrated by the conservative as representing part of Man's collective wealth; it is also a means of encouraging individuals to strive to achieve to better themselves by investing in their unique qualities. The rewards will be theirs to reap. In turn, society will benefit by having its constituents drive to excel in their given fields of expertise and enterprise.

One of the most blatant examples of leftist social reengineering has been the 'affirmative action' agenda. This is the prescriptive practice of redressing one form of institutional bias or disadvantage with another under the guise of providing 'equal opportunity'. In effect it simply swaps one form of alleged discrimination for bureaucratic and administrative injustice, and removes merit and suitability as the pre-eminent decision-making criteria in favour of other factors such as race, gender or religion. Ironically, it discriminates against a target group on exactly the same basis as that target group's alleged discriminatory conduct itself, even while the alleged discrimination is merely presumed for ideological reasons.[14]

History has shown us time and time again that the radical pursuit of justice leads to injustice. This is why *we need a conservative revolution*.

---

14 For example, the bigoted mindset where men or people of European descent are categorically denounced as historical 'oppressors'. This mindset demands that they must have their opportunities limited and penalised by preferencing others in appointments, promotions, admissions and the like. It also demands that the allocation of tax resources to initiatives in health and education largely ignores them and their needs.

## 6. *Principle of imperfectability*

The conservative knows that there is no 'utopia', which, ironically, is a double negative; given that utopia means 'no place'. The idea of the perfect state is a figment of our imagination just as surely as we know that human nature is in itself imperfect. Thomas More, lawyer, statesman and martyr, coined the word 'utopia' in 1516 in an allegorical work based on a perfect island society. 'Progressive' types didn't quite understand it then, and they don't understand it now. Unfortunately, in every society there will be injustice, suffering and maladministration. To expect perfection in our political or social being, and to coerce it when it is not realised, is to risk disorder and chaos. This is because such pursuits seem to lead to the breakdown in the structures that have been established through the experience of past generations. Our forefathers discovered which conduct and what ideas were capable of mediating the imperfect and fallen nature of man. Ignoring their lessons has led to moral anarchy and system failure, and only further highlights the impossibility of forcing Man to be perfect through the coercive fist of executive power.

At its very core, the utopian ideal can never be sustained. Mankind is too restless in spirit to accept the *status quo* for any length of time and will always yearn and advocate change. This change, the conservative argues, should be prudent and considered, lest the solution be worse than the perceived malady.

Too much damage has been done to society and the individual through 'progressive' wishful thinking. This is why *we need a conservative revolution.*

## 7. *Freedom and property*

Property rights are at the very centre of the civic ideal. The unbridled growth of the State invariably and ultimately results in various restrictions on the private ownership of property. This is because there is a heightened temptation for the State to obtain more power and influence over its subjects. This effectively means that executive powers increasingly prevail on the personal affairs of men. Great civilisations are built on the foundation of private ownership as an incentive to encourage economic progress. It is central to the creation of wealth. The centralisation of political and governmental authority is therefore a direct threat to this.

There is a fundamental moral dimension to the principles of the freedom connected to property rights. Private property ownership supports the acceptance of personal responsibility and the importance of pursuing long-term goals. It lifts Man above the day-to-day needs of his own existence and gives him cause to consider the future legacy he will leave his heirs and successors. This is a responsibility that is attached to private ownership and welcomed by those who engage in this basic tenet of freedom.

Those who draft state policy seem to have forgotten these truths. This is why *we need a conservative revolution*.

### 8. *Uphold voluntary community*

A sense of community is pivotal to conservative thought. There is little point talking about 'tradition', 'culture', 'heritage' and a people's 'legacy' without reference to a sense of community, a sense of *peoplehood*. Such things do not exist in a vacuum.

However, the conservative acknowledges that the concept of community cannot be enforced by centralised rule from 'on high'. Community is best fostered when decisions most directly affecting the lives of citizens are taken locally and voluntarily.[15] Sometimes these

---

15 This is often described as the 'principle of subsidiarity', which will be discussed in more detail later in this volume. For an exposition on subsidiarity, see: John Horvat II, *Return to Order* (York Press, 2013) pp. 176, 208-209.

are decisions of a political nature but often they are decisions that can be best made by private organisations or families. Whenever these decisions are subsumed within a larger government, the collective decision is often misguided, ill-informed, and in extreme cases, hostile to personal freedom and human dignity. More often than not, it will lack any depth of commitment precisely because centralised decisions made by some impersonal bureaucracy will most likely disenfranchise and therefore enfeeble communities, organisations and individuals. This is naturally resisted by the conservative as incompatible with local autonomy and individual self-respect. It is resisted because it is, simply, incompatible with reason and human dignity.

This is why *we need a conservative revolution*.

## 9. *Prudent restraint on power*

The two extremes of governance are tyranny (illegitimate governance through overregulation and autocracy) and anarchy (illegitimate governance through negligent and reckless policies that exacerbate Man's fallen nature and encourage social chaos). Neither are acceptable states of being to the conservative mind.

Where a small group of people are allowed to dominate the decision-making process there is risk of tyranny. Conversely, when every individual is a law unto himself, free to indulge in his own appetites without consideration of others, the result is something approaching anarchy.

United States paleoconservative theorist Samuel 'Sam' Francis has even suggested that the two trends can exist in parallel. He refers to this phenomenon as "anarcho-tyranny". According to Francis, in a state of anarcho-tyranny, authorities crack down on the law-abiding citizen with ever intrusive laws and regulations while they become impotent to deal with social dissolution and the very real and much more threatening problems it poses.[16] Perhaps this is because a political elite that has become morally bankrupt and unable to deal with real problems will try to overcompensate by focusing on secondary, perhaps even trivial issues, or invent controversies so as to be seen to 'do something'.

Whatever the reason may be, Francis' anarcho-tyranny concept may have a deeper cause. As early as 1953, Robert Nisbet wrote about how individualism would naturally lead towards centralisation. In general terms, this was because the power of the state would replace local authority (family, guild, etc) once that local authority dissolved. The reason was not so much because of the need to maintain order, but because a people's desire for a sense of belonging and community would incline them to seek out the authority where it was more likely to arise.[17]

Thus the two parallel trends, statist centralisation and individualistic moral anarchy can actually feed off each other, amplifying their worst effects. This can be witnessed when moral anarchy gives state authorities 'reason' to be ever more intrusive in the private affairs of individuals; the intervention itself further demoralises the people, and therefore further encourages the growth of the moral anarchy which the intrusive state seeks to suppress.

It is not surprising that we witness this vicious cycle in the West as our local communities shed their moral traditions. It is the quest of every conservative to pursue a path that will ensure that neither condition, tyranny or anarchy, will develop. Men and women will always strive to gain more power for temporary gain and the

16 Samuel Francis, 'Anarcho-Tyranny, USA', *Chronicles*, vol. 18, no. 7 (July 1994) pp. 14-19. See also Tom Piatak, 'Sam Francis Was Right', *Chronicles*, vol. 36, no. 6 (June 2012) pp. 19-22.
17 Robert Nisbet, *The Quest for Community* (ISI Books, 2010; originally 1953).

conservative knows a limit must be placed on the attainment of such power. This can be achieved through decentralisation of government, checks and balances within the constitution, the enforcement of law and in the maintenance of society's agreed norms and codes of behaviour. These are the conservative's instruments of choice for balancing freedom and order whilst maintaining a prudent progression of society.

How these tools are to be used and the degree of their use may be debated, but what is undoubtedly true today is that the present path we have chosen as a society is leading us towards the kind of anarcho-tyranny which is not conducive to human dignity or social cohesion.

This vicious cycle must be broken if we are to retain a sense of pride and dignity as a nation which is confident with its place in the world. This is why *we need a conservative revolution*.

## 10. *Permanence and change recognised and reconciled*

Radicals will claim that the conservative is opposed to change yet nothing could be further from the truth. The conservative recognises that progress is vital for the ongoing development of civilisation and society. Indeed, a society that is inflexible or which fails to renew itself when necessary is a society doomed to fail. Where the radical and the conservative differ is in their concept of what progress means. Indeed, taking a step forward over a cliff is progress of sorts. But it is not the progress that interests the conservative politician or voter.

The desire for change must be reconciled against the need for the enduring structures, interests and convictions that give us stability and continuity. Protecting these permanent interests is a foil against the threat of society descending into anarcho-tyranny. This timeless wisdom comes to us from ages past: Marcus Aurelius wrote that "to be in the process of change is not an evil, any more than to be a product of change is a good."[18] Thus, whatever is 'new' should be based on proven wisdom rather than idealistic speculation. As is often said: before one moves to knock down a fence, wisdom asks why someone thought to put it there in the first place.

Most people identifying themselves as conservatives will support a number of the principles outlined above. Some may agree with all, most or even just some of them. The fact that such differences exist reinforces the proposition that conservatism is not dogmatic or doctrinaire, but a philosophical state of mind, a disposition, an attitude, a *way of being*.

Thus modern conservatism, while perceived as a counterweight to the political left, is much more than what popular commentators will label 'right-wing' politics. Indeed, the conservative may even reject the 'right-wing' label as being incompatible with freedom, order and the interests of society for the simple reason that conservatism eschews ideological tendencies be they of the left *or the right*.

Yet there are other, equally valid points of view, which may incline even those of conservative disposition towards *reaction*. This is mostly because the radicals of yesteryear seem to have made such progress in reshaping society that these traditionalist conservatives see little in contemporary popular culture worthy of *conservation* and wish to *return to a lost order*. For example, M.E. Bradford wrote that a *reactionary* is "a sensible man who wishes to restore familiar arrangements that worked rather well and have been recently disrupted" and that *reaction* "is a necessary term in the intellectual context we inhabit late in the 20th century because merely to conserve is sometimes to perpetuate what

---

18 Marcus Aurelius, *Meditations*, bk. IV § 42 (Penguin, 1964) p. 74.

is outrageous."[19] It is difficult not to have some sympathy with this view, as we look at the extent of leftist vandalism committed against our culture and civilisation over decades past. Nevertheless, perhaps the most accurate distinction between the two major political actors today was given by Kirk in a lecture to the U.S. Heritage Foundation in 1986:

> The great line of demarcation in modern politics, Eric Voegelin used to point out, is not a division between liberals on one side and totalitarians on the other. No, on one side of that line are all those men and women who fancy that the temporal order is the only order, and that material needs are their only needs, and that they may do as they like with the human patrimony. On the other side of that line are all those people who recognize an enduring moral order in the universe, a constant human nature, and high duties toward the order spiritual and the order temporal.[20]

In other words, the conservative believes that there is something greater over and above himself, and this greater force plays an important role in everyday life, shaping our culture, outlook on the world, our attitude to our neighbours, and our politics. Such a view, such an attitude, is greatly lacking in political discourse today, so-much-so that perhaps it is indeed reactionary to seek its restoration. Anything less than this risks "perpetuating the outrageous" in Bradford's terminology. This is why *we need a conservative revolution.*

---

19 M. E. Bradford, *The Reactionary Imperative* (Sherwood Sugden & Co, 1990) p. ii. In his definition, Bradford draws on the intellectual traditions of Allan Tate and Joshua Asherton. These personalities may be unfamiliar to the Australian reader, but the ideas that are considered by them are no less relevant to us today.
20 Russel Kirk, Heritage Foundation Lecture, (20 March 1986), *op. cit.*

## The challenges ahead

As we face the challenges ahead, there will be an increasing need to ensure that the battleground on which we stand to fight for the things that really matter is solid and dependable; for nothing cruels the opportunity for success as assuredly as a rotting foundation. A fearless and robust conservatism, its actions and beliefs provides for that stability.

Of course, in fighting for these matters of substance, we are not necessarily simply advocating for the *status quo*. In fact, this volume is an exploration of *why we actually need to change the existing order*, to restore the principles, the virtues and values that have served mankind so well over the centuries.

The conservative battle is to restore the foundation of our society by promoting the essential pillars that have given us a national identity, a just and orderly society and confidence in the future.

As illustrated above, conservative policy works to promote these vital pillars by ensuring the wisdom of experience is shared through successive generations. The application of these principles is especially vital in key aspects of our lives.

The chapters in this volume seek to explore these vital pillars and how the resurrection of conservative principles and their application in these key areas can help forge a stronger, more culturally confident as well as politically and economically stable Australia.

Our shared **Faith**, built jointly on the rich heritage of our Greco-Roman philosophy and Judeo-Christian traditions, connects all members of our community in a unique and precious manner. 'Precious' because this legacy is the source of much of our culture, our ideas about what is right and wrong, our concepts of what it means to be human and the ethics of our civil society. The principles faith has provided continue to guide many of our most critical and important decisions. Faith promotes the vital relationship between the individual and society as a whole.

The **Family** is central to most Australians' lives. Strong families are the cornerstone of our communities. They are responsible for raising the next generation and incumbent upon them is the need to act as conduits for the wisdom, the values and the virtues that have allowed society to progress through the ages.

Australia's **Flag** represents our sovereignty, rule of law, Constitution and democracy: the maintenance of which is the government's primary responsibility.

The prosperity we enjoy is not a result of government interference but a direct result of the application of **Free Enterprise** within our economy. By rewarding effort and accepting the consequence of failure, we have established a nation rich in ideas, populated by an industrious people capable of innovation and invention. We can no more afford to stifle that enterprise and expect enduring wealth creation than cease to breathe and expect to stay alive.

These four pillars represent the foundation of an enduring Australia. Without an ongoing commitment to their preservation, the **Freedom** of our citizens and the **Future** of our nation will be at risk.

It is my view that only the traditionalist, conservative approach to public policy properly values these ideas, allowing them to be expressed though responsible governance. This is why *we need a conservative revolution.*

# 2

# The First Pillar: Faith

A ustralia's future will be shaped by the faith of its people. In a world of constant change, direction and clarity have never been more important. Our quest to develop effective policy and promote our nation's interests while limiting government's reach will be stifled without the social unity that faith provides.

It is my hope that Australia's future will be defined, not by excessive government planning and interference, but by the free will and initiative of its people. Nowhere does a society prosper more than in a nation that is free, orderly and built on the shared values that faith provides.

Faith has been part of Australian life from the day our Constitution was proclaimed – indeed, it provided the very foundation of this vital document. The "blessing of Almighty God" which our forebears humbly relied on is still relevant today.[21] Faith and religious observance is maintained by the majority, representing meaningful connection between individuals and their larger concerns of life and its purpose.

The processes that have come to represent this observance – attending church, engaging in prayer and allowing religious principles

---

21 This reference is made in the Preamble to the *Act to Constitute the Commonwealth of Australia* (9 July 1900). It is interesting to note that there was no appeal to God in earlier drafts of proposed constitutions for an Australasian federation; there were however appeals to 'Lords Temporal and Spiritual', which is a reference to the Bishops who sat in the British House of Lords. Religion and religious institutions clearly played an important role in the formation of our national character and the genesis of our state. For more information about the processes involved leading up to federation: John Williams, *The Australian Constitution – A Documentary History* (Melbourne University Press, 2005).

to inform one's judgment – should not be ridiculed or dismissed as out of touch or archaic. Indeed, they are part of a foundation of considered action that is in many ways preferable to rash, tokenistic judgments which are often guided more by populist sentiment than substantive thought.

But faith is more than simply a belief in a greater being. Even the non-religious demonstrate a kind of faith through belief in their country, their leaders, themselves and their fellow man. History has shown that faith provides people with hope, and this is especially the case during difficult times. It acts as a guide and a framework within which decisions can be made. As a nation we cannot afford to lose faith. To do so would be to remove the common thread through which our laws, our instinct and our social fabric are entwined.

The question then remains, where does faith come from and what can be done to sustain it?

## Where does faith come from?

In tracing the origin of faith in our community, it would be easy to look through the great volumes of history, formulating a timeline of Christian thought and reproducing it here. However, to do so would have little relevance to the real task at hand which is to examine how individuals today develop their faith.

I believe the answer to that is within the family.

Some children grow up in a family that follows the ethical principles of an organised religion. Accordingly, they develop their moral guidelines within the framework of those teachings.

Others may be encouraged by their parents to develop a set of values based not on a particular religious figure but built around personal integrity, kindness, hard work and the natural law.

The common thread between these two different approaches is the importance of moral standards. These will be the standards that young people carry with them as they enter adulthood and will be the standards that they will ultimately share with their children. After all, as C.S. Lewis observed, the "mind has no more power of inventing a new value than of imagining a new colour, or, indeed, of creating a new sun and a new sky for it to move in."[22] In other words, moral order has its genesis in belief in God; otherwise, why would we bother trying to lead moral lives and why, indeed, are basic moral standards universal?

The diminution of faith in our community bears a direct relationship to the hesitance by many parents (as well as church and other community leaders) to draw clear distinctions between what is right and wrong. Both are cause and both are effect.

We have become a society where there is an excuse for every transgression, and a new 'disorder' is seemingly diagnosed every day for almost every aspect of poor behaviour.

In times past, an overactive child would be encouraged to work some energy off in the playground or on the sports field or be taught the importance of good behaviour through example or discipline. Today, that same child may be prescribed as having some new condition and given a course of drugs to keep them quiet and docile.

To question the wisdom of that approach is not to decry the important advances in modern medicine. However, it seems that rather than accept the responsibilities of disciplining children and teaching them right from wrong, too many parents are indulging their children's poor behaviour while conveniently assuming the premise that they are suffering some newly diagnosable imbalance or dysfunction. Our education and social welfare systems by and large seem to support this attitude.

---

22 C. S. Lewis, *The Abolition of Man* (McMillan, 1973) pp. 156-157.

We must not neglect the task of passing on critical values to our children. The explicit and implicit codes (what we sometimes called 'taboos') arising from a duty to others and to God which were passed down to us, were always seen as a moderating influence upon our freedoms. They were the glue that drew us together to form and maintain our society under the principle of 'the common good.' Faith in a compassionate and tolerant society has served us well. Respect for and belief in our fellow man are the hallmarks of our community. The religious traditions we have inherited from our forefathers have provided a guide for good behaviour and good citizenship. Thus, even in a secular nation, one cannot dismiss the positive role that our particular religious values and traditions have played in shaping our world and our society.

These have played a vital role in our national development; without them, we risk losing our historic and moral anchor. I believe that only a government which understands the value of our past can truly appreciate the value of the most important institution of cultural transmission: the family. This is why *we need a conservative revolution.*

### The Christian tradition and the values we derive from it are the foundation of Australian society

Australia is a secular country but it is, at the same time, a Christian nation. Nearly two-thirds of her citizens identify themselves as Christian. Although this number has been falling slowly in recent years, little over seven per cent of the total population identify themselves with non-Christian religions.[23]

---

23 Australian Bureau of Statistics, 2012, *Reflecting a Nation: Stories from the 2011 Census, 2012-13,* cat no. 2071.0 – Cultural Diversity in Australia, viewed 23 July 2013, <www.abs. gov.au/ausstats/abs@.nsf/Lookup/2071.0main+features902012-2013>; see the table and commentary on 'religious affiliation' therein.

That said, the overwhelming majority of Australians identify with the principles and values that have been established by the historical religious traditions on which this country has been built. These traditions have codified the natural law within our laws and our social conventions. As a result, even those who are not Christian, or who may have no religious loyalties or connections, will likely identify with values that would not exist if it weren't for the historical role that Christianity has played in shaping the cultural background of Australia and the greater Western civilisation it is part of.

While some aspects of this tradition are more contentious than others, the values at the very heart of our nation spring from the concept of human dignity, liberty and compassion. It is difficult to imagine an ardent secularist, or even a militant atheist arguing against these concepts. "Even secular democracy is workable only on the basis of Christian assumptions about human dignity, respect for persons, natural rights, the common good", writes George Cardinal Pell, adding that "[t]hese principles do not come about simply by bringing people together in a community."[24] Indeed, the very idea of secular equality can be harmful if it is divorced from the moral foundations out of which liberal society has come to celebrate it as a value.[25]

Earlier I wrote that the "quest to remove all inequality is the deadening hand of socialism". It might seem strange then that I am defending the concept of equality as one of the founding values of Australian society. In this context, I am referring to the *equal moral worth of every person*; our *innate and inalienable dignity* that we all share in *equal*

---

24 George Pell, *God and Caesar – Selected Essays on Religion, Politics and Society* (Connor Court and the Catholic University of America, 2007) p. 53.

25 A recent work about the inextricable connection between Christianity and Western civilisation, which I recommend particularly to young readers, is Dinesh D'Souza, *What's So Great About Christianity* (Regnery, 2007), in particular pt. II 'Christianity and the West', pt. V 'Christianity and Philosophy' and pt. VII 'Christianity and Morality'.

*measure*. This idea of equality is founded in the Christian belief that God values every individual human life because Man "was created in the image of God".[26] With some notable and unfortunate exceptions which will be discussed later, this is reflected in our society today and is inconceivable without the moral and therefore specifically Christian religious traditions of the West.

The very notion of true liberty is often difficult to grasp because it tends to be measured according to subjective values that can differ widely between individuals and cultures. When it is appealed to, it often seems connected to the idea of personal freedom. One might argue that freedom itself can never be absolute as the inevitable result of unfettered or unconstrained behaviour will be one individual trespassing on the liberty of another. However, within a framework of laws and ethical boundaries, a maximum practical level of freedom can be obtained. In fact, freedom without such boundaries is no freedom at all, at least it is not freedom in any meaningful sense.

The framework of our Western moral tradition can be found in the wisdom of the Ten Commandments, and the lessons of Christ and the life of the Apostles. Thus, secular or not, our society is based on the principles of religious faith, borne of the natural law that is engraved on our very heart, reflected in our customs and codified in our laws.

I believe that only a traditionalist-minded government can appreciate the importance and need for these principles, and this is why *we need a conservative revolution*.

---

26 This is the doctrine of *Imago Dei* which can be found in the first Book of the Old Testament and is repeated in the New Testament at 1 Cor 11:7 and James 3:9. The Christian concept of human dignity is largely derived from the idea that Man is created in the image of God.

## How religious faith informs our principles

There are some who will mock or belittle organised religion and the conviction of the religious faithful. Indeed there is a very vocal minority who have sought to replace the Christian faith with almost any alternative. But this comes at a high risk and should be a source of concern to all men of reason: as was once observed, "those who do not believe in God, will believe in anything"![27] This must be resisted by the conservative whether or not they are religious themselves.

It should come as no surprise that Christianity, which is at the very heart of Western culture, should be attacked and derided by cultural Marxists. In its attempts to undermine that most enduring set of beliefs which support Man's pursuit of a nobler purpose (other than mere base, personal gratification), cultural Marxism has been one of the most corrosive influences on society over the last century. The reasons for this have been known to those who struggled with the aimlessness and nihilism that plagued their societies of centuries past: Seneca the Younger once wrote that "if one does not know to which port one is sailing, no wind is favourable."[28]

I believe that by stripping God and religious principles from our culture (and our politics) we have become a nation which does not know what port it is sailing to. Without the notion of the transcendent in our daily and public lives, we will undoubtedly lose a sense of the profound. Such a loss is like a killing of the spirit of civilisation.

The weapons of choice of the cultural assassins are drawn from the arsenal of the 'counter-culture' movement that has taken hold in many of our contemporary institutions of cultural transmission. The

---

27 This quote is often attributed to G.K. Chesterton and can be found in various forms throughout his work.

28 Lucius Annaeus Seneca ('Seneca the Younger', circa 4BC to 65AD) *Epistulae Morales ad Lucilium* bk. LXXI § 3.

media, our universities and public school system all contribute to the assault on the core civilising functions of our social mores.

For decades now, the traditional values we have long held dear have been under attack and deemed to be 'oppressive.' The values that always determined good from bad, right from wrong and just from unjust have fallen away as their foundations have been undermined and weakened. Whenever these cultural Marxists failed to convince (usually because they wanted too much, too soon), they simply changed tack, falling back, more often than not, upon the hoary shibboleths of 'choice', a crude understanding of 'freedom' and human rights. The sins of generations past have somehow become the 'virtues' of today and what were previously regarded as virtues have too frequently become cause for condemnation.

The results seem to be dire indeed. The principles of hard work and persistence have been lost to an entire generation, replaced with fast money, materialism and an addiction to debt. Monogamy and a commitment to family life are deemed unfashionable and antiquated. Marriage is decried by some social commentators as being akin to slavery for women rather than an enduring commitment of love and support between man and woman.[29] There are even demands (and acceptance in some countries) for same-sex marriage as a 'right'.

These are just a few examples of how the culture wars have eroded the principles attached to our moral heritage, and this is why *we need a conservative revolution.*

---

29 For example, Germaine Greer argued in her 1970 work *The Female Eunuch* that "[i]f women are to effect a significant amelioration in their condition it seems obvious that they must refuse to marry." (see Harper Perennial, 2008 ed. at p. 358). Indeed, one of the most prominent 'progressive' politicians in the United States today, Hillary Clinton once famously put marriage in the same category as slavery in an article about dependency arrangements. See 'Do First Ladies' Views Matter?' *Chicago Tribune* (online) (16 August 1992) <www.chicagotribune.com> (accessed 22 August 2013). Print edition not available to the writer.

## Culture wars

Conservatives have been losing the battle for our culture because we haven't been sufficiently prepared to affirm and defend it. The defence of our culture begins with the affirmation of the bedrock of our Christian values, for reasons already articulated above.

It is no coincidence that, as the attack on our moral customs and traditions has gained momentum, our society has experienced an overall state of decline. Noticeable symptoms include a general sense of detachment from community, a reduced level of public service, higher crime rates, increasing levels of poor health, loneliness, relationship breakdown and child abuse.[30] The culture of drug and alcohol abuse, for example, is creating inter-generational problems as the line between right and wrong becomes too blurred for many to see; their stupor being itself a powerful metaphor.

Unfortunately, it seems as if dysfunction has now become the norm rather than the exception. In our 'pop' culture, it has even become a focus of endearing humour; honesty and sincerity has become naïve, even an embarrassment or a weakness; promiscuity is expected among both our young men and women, and those

30 Australian Bureau of Statistics 2013, 'Increased physical assaults in 2011-12' media release, 19 February 2013 <www.abs.gov.au> (accessed 26 July 2013). Nino Bucci, 'Police grapple with challenges as crime rate rises', *The Age* (online) (1 March 2013) <www.theage.com.au> (accessed 26 July 2013) Print edition not available to writer. Marissa Calligeros, 'Queensland crime rate spikes', *Brisbane Times* (online) (24 October 2012) <www.brisbanetimes.com.au> (accessed 25 July 2013) Print edition not available to writer. Department of Prime Minister and Cabinet, Families in Australia: 2008, PM&C, Canberra, p. 11. Lixia Qu and Ruth Weston, 'Trends in couple dissolution: an update', *Family Relationships Quarterly* No. 19, Child Family Community Australia (2011) <www.aifs.gov.au/cfca> (accessed 24 July 2013). Australian Institute of Family Studies (as updated by Deborah Scott), 'Child abuse and neglect statistics' (May 2013) <www.aifs.gov.au> (accessed 21 July 2013); this paper is a summary of pertinent data which appeared in the following report: *Australian Institute of Health and Welfare, Child Protection Australia 2011-2012*, Child Welfare Series No. 55, Catalogue CWS 43 (release dated 8 March 2013).

who don't dance to the 'progressive' tune are considered odd or strange.

All this can be redressed with a stronger commitment to the principles espoused by the Christian faith at the very centre of our culture. The principles which have guided mankind for centuries provide a very clear map of the path we should take. In fact, they should be entirely uncontroversial for the religious *and non-religious alike*.

This last point is a very important one, and needs to be emphasised and re-emphasised by the faithful at every opportunity. A frequently encountered retort to the religious citizen is that his opinions are irrational, based on superstitions, fundamentally unscientific and therefore illegitimate, unworthy of serious attention. Yet as we see the desolate wasteland of destruction strewn across last century, we cannot but notice that the overwhelming majority of those atrocities were committed in the name of ideologies dedicated to pure science and rationality, from Nazism to Soviet and Chinese Communism.

Why did this pure science and rationality lead to such a nightmare century? Because it lacked a conscience that only an appreciation of a higher moral order can provide. On the balance sheet of humanity, it does not appear that the secular left has all that much it can teach us, unless it is a lesson of mistakes to avoid. Indeed, there is nothing more *reasonable* than to preserve the Christian worldview on which the foundation of the West depends and promote it to the next generation within our families, in our schools, universities, our media, and yes, our politics too.

By restoring moral responsibility, a belief in the innate value of every human life, the importance of respect, love and honour, believing in a greater being than oneself, treating others as you would like to be treated, not stealing, lying or cheating – we will have the recipe for a safer and more successful society. Of course, all these precepts can be rationalised without reference to Christianity or religion; nevertheless they are fundamentally based on that uniquely Christian doctrine of *Imago Dei*, or that "man was created in the image of God," a principle on which the Western concept of human dignity ultimately depends. Without it, that same secular ideologue would just as easily rationalise the 'right' of the state to unjustly appropriate property, redistribute wealth, or kill the unborn (to name just a few heated controversies of the day).

Reversing the decline and decay of our culture must be the first priority of the 'conservative revolution.' Without a strategy for restoring our nation to its rightful and sustainable path, we risk bearing witness to, and being a part of, the very dismantling of Western culture.

Of course, this clarion call will be rejected by the cultural Marxists who seek to control almost every aspect of our society. They will no doubt consider it a direct assault on their *raison d'être*, whereas the conservative would consider it the defence of the eternal truths that are at the very core of Western civilisation.

If we truly have an interest in the future of our nation, we cannot allow these cultural vandals to have their way unopposed. This is why *we need a conservative revolution.*

## Know thine enemy!

Before we can work on defending and promoting our culture, we first need to recognise the genesis of this cultural vandalism in the various communistic movements after the First World War.

According to post-war Marxist theorists Antonio Gramsci and George Lukács, for communism to succeed in the West, broadly speaking Christianity and the traditions of Western culture had to first be undermined and ultimately destroyed. The first target in the crosshairs were the traditional sexual mores of the West. The first salvo was the introduction of sex education in Soviet Hungary's public school system.

This initial 'success' inspired other Marxists to establish the Institute for Social Research at Frankfurt University; better known as the 'Frankfurt School.' This was where the concept of 'political correctness' was born; an insidious doctrine that has led an assault on our culture ever since and has made its presence felt in social and political discourse on almost any subject today.

The Frankfurt School encouraged a revolution led by the 'victims' of an oppressive society. Minority groups, some of whom had legitimate grievances, became the vocal revolutionaries, demanding the old structures be dismantled to protect their rights.

No matter how well they functioned, there was unrelenting criticism of the traditional family, authority and our social structure. Those who believed in and supported traditional Western culture were branded 'racist,' 'intolerant,' 'homophobic,' 'sexist' and 'prejudiced.' It should come as no surprise that those whose argument has no substance are reduced to make *ad hominem* attacks on their opponents. Through seemingly endless public attacks on our social traditions, many of which were uncontested lest the defender become a target for leftist vitriol himself, the public conditioning continued without the clarity of rational debate.

Soon the concept of 'repressive' or 'liberating tolerance' was formulated by another member of the Frankfurt School, Herbert Marcuse.[31] This was defined as tolerance for all ideas from the left of

---

31 For a discussion of this, see: Rolf Wiggerhause (eng. tr. Michael Robertson), *The Frankfurt School – its History, Theories and Political Significance* (MIT Press, 2007; originally in German, Carl Hanser Verlag, 1986) pp. 611-612.

the political spectrum and intolerance for any ideas coming from the right, essentially because all non-'progressive' ideas were denounced as oppressive and therefore illegitimate – violence against them was not immoral. Not surprisingly, other members of the Frankfurt School would lay the groundwork for the belief among many radicals of today that people of conservative disposition are in fact morally or psychologically defective in some way.[32]

One consequence of this debilitating mindset is the stranglehold that leftist taboos and politically correct notions have on public debate today. This stranglehold has influenced the media, and through it, the political establishment itself. In 2010, traditionalist commentator Edwin Dyga wrote about the harmful affect this has had on the state of democracy, where the oppressive culture of leftist prejudice has significantly impoverished political choice, especially for conservative voters:

> Without substantive political alternatives, democracy then becomes a purely procedural affair; a battle of brands and personalities instead of ideas and competing philosophies; the administrative technique of a multi-party yet mono-ideological managerial class. As a consequence, it is reasonable to predict a gradual drift away from the political and media mainstream by a growing portion of a disaffected electorate. This is especially the case for traditionalist conservatives who find it increasingly difficult to accept a "centre" that appears to be constantly relocating towards the left.[33]

Dyga refers to the process where conservative thought gradually

---

32 Theodor Adorno, Else Frenkel-Brunswik, Daniel Levinson and Nevitt Sanford, *The Authoritarian Personality* (Harper & Row, 1950).
33 Edwin Dyga, 'The Rise of Conservative Dissent in the Blogosphere'. *Quadrant*, vol. LIV, no. 9(469) (September 2010) p. 43. Also available fully referenced and in two parts online at <www.quadrant.org.au>, see pt 1 at ¶ 22.

assimilates to essentially leftist ideas as 'cognitive harmonisation'. Marcuse's concept of 'tolerance', together with a timid political opposition to it, has led to the situation we find ourselves in today. The resulting alienation of voters from those who are supposed to represent them in parliament should be worrying to anyone with an interest in maintaining representative government or public involvement in the political process. Dyga's observations reinforce the present need for a conservative revolution which rejects the Frankfurt School's ideas of 'tolerance', so that people can discuss matters without fear of leftist slander, and so a *genuine political choice* can be available to the voter come election time.

Unfortunately, such was the Frankfurt School's success that this concept of 'repressive tolerance' continues today, with no better example than the irrational hysteria attached to (among many other things) the modern green fad of the anthropogenic global warming theory. We witnessed this recently with the fiasco of 'Climategate,' when the gross impropriety of scientists who promoted the theory as partial agents in what was obviously a political campaign to fool the public, were shielded by a cowardly and compliant leftist media.[34]

It is perhaps telling that the process of secularisation (where traditional religious principles and ideas have gradually been eradicated from the public arena all in the name of science, reason and rationality) has paralleled the growth of the near cultish obsession with militant green environmentalism, sometimes even bordering on Earth worship. Chesterton has again been proven right. Green-left ideologues' frequent critique of the materialism of the free market is strong evidence of their desire for some kind of *transcendent purpose* in

---

34 'Climategate' occurred when thousands of emails and documents from the Climatic Research Unit at the University of East Anglia were leaked online. See John Costella (ed.), *The Climategate Emails* (The Lavoisier Group, 2010).

life. Unfortunately, they have rejected the very religious and cultural heritage that was best equipped to satisfy this deep rooted need. The result is that they will fall for anything, just as Chesterton predicted. And here Burke too is vindicated: he suspected that the alternative to our Christian heritage would be "some uncouth, pernicious, and degrading superstition."[35]

It is not surprising that in this ideologically charged environment, where dissent is treated like political heresy, free thought and expression would surely suffer. Thus the outlandish claims of celebrity scientists about 'inevitable' sea level rises, uninhabitable cities and the like went largely unchallenged and thus crept into orthodoxy, repeated endlessly in the media, our educational institutions and by government.

As the demand for action to avert catastrophic global warming grew apace, a few scientists dared challenge the statements of the alarmists. When it was pointed out that some of the outlandish global warming claims were demonstrably false, the questioners became the persecuted.

Publicly accused of being deniers and heretics, many were browbeaten into submission. However, a brave few persisted and dared to claim *locus standii* in the debate using logic and evidence against the emotional blackmail of the alarmists.

Labelled "the great moral challenge of our generation" by political leaders,[36] the global warming 'debate' has diverted attention away from the necessary discussions we should be having about the

35 Edmund Burke, *Reflections on the Revolution in France* (1790) as published by Penguin in 2004, p. 188.
36 This phrase was popularised by Labor Prime Minister Kevin Rudd during the debate about the proposed creation of a national emissions trading scheme. It has since been a point of ridicule after Rudd's subsequent policy reversal, and the opportunistic way it was dealt with by the former Commonwealth Labor governments.

restoration of the true moral responsibilities that have been lost over recent decades. It is the modern version of 'bread and circuses,' and a distraction from serious debates about matters of far greater social and political importance that we should be discussing instead.

This is not to say that the conservative has no interest in the preservation of the environment,[37] but the leftist moral panics, fostered by a shrill and partisan press, do nothing to help create a responsible policy framework to protect natural resources and our beautiful ecology. This is why *we need a conservative revolution*.

## Moral responsibility – the Moses Code

It is always difficult to define a set of moral codes that we should all adhere to. Certainly, the tenets of the Ten Commandments act as a bedrock guide of how we should strive to live our lives even if circumstances make strict observance difficult at times.

For example, the request to keep the Sabbath holy is a good and worthy aim. It reminds us to reflect on our belief in God and to share time with our friends and loved ones. It is an eternal reminder of the need for balance and reflection in our lives.

However, in our decidedly secular world, it isn't always possible to adhere to the doctrine of scripture. We could identify the many merits of a return to a simpler time, such as when stores were closed on Sundays, but today it would seem impractical to many to suggest a return to those norms.

Regardless, the principle of keeping a day aside to share and love and reflect and worship is an enduring one, the restoration of which would benefit our families and societies immensely.

---

37 For a conservative view of environmentalism, see Roger Scruton, *Green Philosophy* (Atlantic Books, 2012).

Those who challenge the reality that our Western worldview is infused with a behavioural code that stems from our Christian ethos would quickly point out that individuals are largely free to decide how they live their lives and to set their own moral standards, and many choose standards that do not accord with Christian morality. This is true to a point but only because the Christian worldview holds that virtue, to be truly virtuous, must be voluntary.[38] Hence, Christian societies will often have dissenting groups living amongst them, people who do not subscribe to all or even any of the doctrines of the majority or dominant faith. People's choices should remain theirs to make within the existing legal and moral framework. The nature of Christianity makes this possible and successful. But that does not mean that a society which exists under a certain ethos does not have a moral right to maintain and promote that ethos within its legal order, *especially if that order has been tried and proven to be fruitful and conducive to the health of the community and its individual members*. Therein lies the legitimacy of our cause.

Thus, where those choices breach societal expectations or trespass on our traditional customs, they should not be defended as simply 'freedom of choice.' Instead they need to be identified correctly as a challenge to our culture and values.

As such, the conservative will need to speak out to defend *and affirm* the existing culture, lest only the cultural Marxist voice be heard. This is why *we need a conservative revolution*.

### Sanctity of life

There needs to be a vocal defence of traditional values in many areas of society. The most pressing defence is most certainly the defence

---

38 This is inherited from the Aristotelian tradition concerning the exercise of choice: Aristotle (b. 384BC d. 322BC), *Nicomachean Ethics* (written circa 350BC), bk.III.

of life itself against the creeping culture of death that is permeating society.

At one level we have correctly denounced the treatment of human beings as chattels and commodities. The acknowledgment of the equal dignity of all humanity, the abolition of slavery and the granting of equal civil rights to all people regardless of race, creed and colour have been important steps forward in the process of civilisation.

Regretfully though, despite these advances, our society has taken many steps backwards in other areas regarding the right to life and the dignity of the individual. This has perhaps been one of the most glaring and obvious ironies of leftist political thought.

Abortion is effectively available on demand in most Australian states and territories. Morally offensive laws that force doctors to refer patients for abortions, even if they have a conscientious objection to the procedure, have been passed in the state of Victoria.[39] These laws also allow an unborn child to be killed *in utero* after 24 weeks, well past the time when life can be sustained outside of the womb.[40]

While the very mention of abortion evokes passionate responses from both sides of the divide, I don't think that anyone could have imagined forty years ago when legal medical abortion was introduced that this death industry would grow to despatch somewhere between 80,000 to 100,000 unborn children every year. Accurate statistics, however, are very difficult to calculate because of problems associated with the collection of data.[41] Nevertheless, I suspect even a so-called

---

39 Section 8(1)(b) *Abortion Law Reform Act 2008 (Vic)*, as in force at July 2013.
40 *Ibid.*, generally ss. 4 to 7.
41 Victorian Law Reform Commission, *Law of Abortion: Final Report* (1 January 2008) ¶ 8.192. This report refers to Angela Pratt, Amanda Briggs and Luke Buckmaster, Australian Parliamentary Library Research Brief, 'How Many Abortions Are There Each Year in Australia?' (2005).

'pro-choice' activist, assuming they have an ounce of compassion in their hearts, will be forced to conclude that such figures are absolutely horrendous and unacceptable.

In a culture where rights are demanded for every triviality, and a 'Bill of Rights' is advocated by many among the elite, how can they so conveniently ignore the fundamental right to life? Perhaps if an unborn child looked more like a tree or a whale, maybe then the green left would look on it with more sympathy, and even become an advocate for its right to live!

But for some, aborting unborn children is not enough.

Peter Singer, philosopher and co-founder of the Australian Greens, has claimed that even newborn children are not sentient beings for some days and thus can be killed, and such views have been supported by allegedly serious academics presently teaching at universities in Australia.[42] For example, Alberto Giubilini (from Charles Sturt University) and Francesca Minerva (from the University of Melbourne) have jointly argued in the *Journal of Medical Ethics* that killing a child is not immoral, even assuming the 'potential' personhood of a baby.[43] That article is brief, but the abstract alone says it all:

> Abortion is largely accepted even for reasons that do not
> have anything to do with the fetus' health. By showing that
> (1) both fetuses and newborns do not have the same moral
> status as actual persons, (2) the fact that both are potential
> persons is morally irrelevant and (3) adoption is not always

---

42 Peter Singer, *Practical Ethics* (3rd ed., Cambridge University Press, 2011) pp. 159-167.
43 Alberto Giubilini and Francesca Minerva 'After-birth Abortion: Why Should the Baby Live?' *J Med Ethics* (2012) [doi:10.1136/medethics-2011-100411]. Giubilini and Minerva rely in part on the work of Peter Singer, specifically his (together with Helga Kuhse) *Should The Baby Live – The Problem of Handicapped Infants* (Oxford, 1988).

in the best interest of actual people, the authors argue that what we call 'after-birth abortion' (killing a newborn) should be permissible in all the cases where abortion is, including cases where the newborn is not disabled.[44]

Note the language being used here: 'actual persons' and 'actual people.' I believe it is concerning when a serious journal will consider publishing views that seriously question whether or not a human being's humanity is 'actual.' When a pregnant woman is greeted by her friend, what kind of exchange can we expect to occur? Is it more likely one asks the other 'how is your baby doing?' or asks 'how is your potential person?' Even if the women are 'pro-choice' (i.e., pro-death), I think one does not have to be a conservative or even a Christian to know the answer. The fact is that the so-called pro-choice movement is disingenuous and the language it uses is designed to mislead the public and shroud the issue in ambiguity. The fact that they need to do this is perhaps evidence of their insecurity and, deep down in their hearts, a lack of sincere belief in the truth of their position.

It is reassuring to note that the community remains sickened by the concept of legalised infanticide, but it remains of concern that there is a growing group of supporters for such violent actions. Left unchallenged, views like Singer's will find their way into mainstream advocacy and another important threshold regarding the sanctity of life will have been breached. It continues to amaze me that doyens of death like Singer gain unfettered access to the media in this country without anything like the criticism they deserve for their outrageous positions on any number of subjects.

Fr. Paul Marx OSB, at the height of the abortion debates in the United States, predicted that the disregard for the sanctity of life in

---

44 *Ibid.*

the womb would inexorably lead to the same disregard at the other end of life's spectrum. In his acceptance speech for the first Faithful for Life Award in 2004, he said that "I've always said, if you can be killed before birth, why not after?"[45] In some countries people now have the right to die through state-sanctioned suicide. In actual fact, suicide is the wrong term as the proposed lethal cocktail of chemicals, in many instances, will be administered by a third party, often with the consent of the patient.

Alarmingly, the Australian euthanasia lobby claim widespread public support for the introduction of state-sanctioned killings. Their political champions regularly introduce legislation into parliaments around the country seeking to make it legal.

The fact that there does appear to be public support for the endorsement of the state for taking a human life should be worrying in itself. But even ignoring the moral objections to such legislation, it gives rise to a host of other concerns as well, not least of which is the question of how the necessary safety controls (that the euthanasia advocates assure us will protect the vulnerable) are to be maintained.

Already we are seeing evidence of a breach of these safety controls in countries that allow euthanasia. In Belgium, for example, a study revealed that there have been cases of euthanasia carried out without the explicit request of the patient and there have been cases where nurses have administered the lethal dose to patients, despite this being illegal.[46]

The evidence of incremental change to whatever limits we have legislatively placed on ourselves abounds. Where once abortion was

45 *Population Research Institute Review* vol. 14 no. 5 (September/October 2004) <pop.org> (accessed 6 July 2013). Print edition not available to the writer.
46 Alex Schadenberg, *Exposing Vulnerable People to Euthanasia and Assisted Suicide* (Connor Court, 2013) pp. 5-16.

rare and only performed in extreme cases, it is now an abhorrent form of birth control for some women. We have a variety of politicians, philosophers, academics and the public claiming the state-sanctioned need to be able to end life pre-birth, post-birth and in our advanced years. Based on previous experience, it will now only be a matter of time before the earlier and later dates start being drawn closer together through ever more implausible reasons.

Rational and reasoned arguments will of course be used to legitimise this gradual legislative process, and those who oppose it will predictably be denounced as irrational and unreasoned, providing further evidence of that 'repressive tolerance' that dissenters from the liberal *status quo* have grown all too familiar with today. How did a society that once venerated the newborn and the aged, that cared for the disabled, sick and dying, get to the point where we now think it is better to kill them?

The only answer can be that we have lost our moral compass as we have ceased to draw a clear distinction between right and wrong. Like the frog in the pot, which is slowly cooked to death because it doesn't notice the slowly heating water (until it's too late, of course), the incremental nature of the assaults on human life has gone largely unnoticed or unchallenged. Can we afford to be as apathetic as that frog? It is heartening to note Australian Medicare statistics show that women are increasingly rejecting the abortion rebate.[47] This suggests that there is a hopeful trend among young women towards life.

Nevertheless, the political pressure from the left is relentless, and has ushered us into a morbid new world. We abort children *in utero*, we witness apparently intelligent academics argue that killing an infant is not objectionable, we see laws passed to enable euthanasia, we witness

---

47 See: Australian Medicare Benefit Schedule Item No. 35643. For example, the trend can be clearly seen in the recent period since 2000.

the rejection of the inherent dignity of Man through the rejection of the Christian morals that underpin our true human rights. What can we expect on the horizon? Perhaps one day, some 'progressive', efficient, rational radical may decide that you're more trouble than you're worth to the state, and then where will you be? Remember, not too long ago, much of what is being lobbied for by the 'progressive' left was unspeakable, unthinkable nonsense. Today, if you oppose it, you're a bigot.

It's not enough to stop the trend. What is needed is a *reversal* back to sanity and reason, and this is why *we need a conservative revolution.*

## Faith in traditions that have served us well

Faith is much more than an understanding or appreciation of what is right and wrong in any given situation, or the tenets of a particular religious system.

So far, I believe I have argued that there is good reason for our people to have continuing faith in the wisdom of our traditions and the role these traditions have in the continuity of our society and nation. Traditions are valuable, if for no other reason than they have stood the test of time; they are, in the words of John Kekes cited earlier, "the tried and true." They reflect the accumulated wisdom and experience of preceding generations. Or as Chesterton once put it:

> Tradition refuses to submit to the small and arrogant oligarchy of those who merely happen to be walking around. All democrats object to men being disqualified by the accident of birth; tradition objects to their being disqualified by the accident of death.[48]

To put it in simpler terms, we rely on our habits, accepted

---

48 Gilbert Keith Chesterton, *Orthodoxy* (Hendrickson, 2006; originally 1908) p. 43.

standards and customs for the smooth running of our social society, our commerce and our government. This is because these habits, customs and accepted standards represent modes of behaviour that have proven themselves capable of successfully dealing with life's trials.

History is a record of the rapid and often violent changes that society has suffered over time. The 20th century is arguably one of the most dramatic episodes in the history of the West, littered as it is with catastrophic social, political and economic upheavals. Rapid industrialisation, the First and Second World Wars, the Cold War, the sexual revolution of the 1960s, rapid globalisation, the rise of the welfare state and the existential threats posed by militant liberalism at home and Islamic Jihad abroad (and at home now too) have all left their mark on us. People feel disconnected, aimless, question their very identity as often if not more so than previous generations, and have gradually lost faith in themselves and confidence in their place in the world. We are all still grappling with the consequences of these events and trends, and they show no sign of abating.

Although times have changed, the perennial questions about the nature of Man and society are still unanswered and debates continue to rage on these and related topics. What is it to be Man? Are we merely wealth creating and wealth consuming creatures? Is material efficiency the only measure of progress? What is it that is worth living *for*? Are we all fungible, or is there something particular to us, our time and place? Why are we so caught up in life's routines, for what *reason*? How are these things to be reflected in our laws and government policy?

Those who came before us may not have had the benefits (and risks) of modern technology, but the lessons they learned are not without value when we face these same unanswered questions. Is it not prudent, reasonable and rational to consider their experiences as we approach the challenges of the future? I believe that a healthy respect for tradition is the most *genuinely progressive* attitude any citizen can have today.

To ignore the experience of previous generations is to commit to repeating their mistakes. This is entirely unnecessary and is borne more of the radical's refusal to acknowledge that the many goods that evolved, actually evolved before their life began, and that any problems we face today are not to be solely ascribed to any specific failure of our ancestors. The radical's attitude is arrogance *par excellence*.

But the structures and tradition of our culture will only provide the framework on which we can build our conservative future. In order to do so, there is another type of faith we must harness to restore the proven values and virtues associated with the conservative revolution. This is why *we need a conservative revolution*.

## Faith as an instrument to avoid downfall

Faith provides a structure to the belief that there is more to life than self-gratification. The concept that there is something greater than self is a very humbling one. In some it manifests itself as belief in God; in others, a sense of community or familial responsibility; or a combination of all three.

A commitment to the greater good acts as a foil to the temptation to ignore our proven values system in search of ego-driven temporal satisfaction. Such personal pursuits may, for a time, seem to result in success, but there is always a larger cost involved in pursuing the banal.

For individuals, the cost may be in terms of their health and wellbeing. Stress, mental illness and physical disease are often a result of the pressures we place upon ourselves in pursuit of what we deem to be important. But in a hyper materialist environment where everything is reduced to mere economic considerations, what we deem to be important is often trivial, a temporary fix for deeper and more profound yearnings. This has given rise to what some may describe as a unique pathology common to modern wealthy societies: moral and spiritual emptiness among opulence and material luxury.

The desire for a larger house, more money, a new car and trying to 'keep up with the Joneses' can literally be debilitating for some people. Why is it that after so much radical 'progress' in social policy we still have such high rates of sadness and depression, particularly among our youth? Something essential is obviously missing in their lives, but do not expect the radical to tell you what it is. The left is known for many things, but admitting to their errors is not one of them.

Invariably, what may once have been thought of as important seems less so when considered within the context of collective social ill health. This is where the notion of community service plays an important role. Time serving one's fellow citizens as a volunteer, helper, group leader or almost any other role allows people to experience life from someone else's perspective. It also fosters a sense of rootedness and belonging to a greater whole, and for this reason, gives purpose to an individual's life. From this, it is a short step towards fostering hope for the future, and therefore self-motivated initiative. Participation in one's local community is therefore the bedrock on which good citizenship and patriotism can be built.

A scoutmaster will be brought into contact with children who face serious disadvantage. The 'Meals on Wheels' volunteer will see first-hand the impoverished and infirm in our communities. They will also experience the wonderful gratitude, kindness and generosity of those who often give as much as they can. Similar benefits will be gained from almost all forms of community service.

Experience with others who are less well-off can make an individual grateful for what he actually has. Sharing experiences with those who have more can serve as personal inspiration, which ultimately may lead a person to inspire others. Such is the nature of making a contribution to the local community. It acts as an effective antidote to both excessive pessimism and hubris.

Parents, too, practise a form of community service when they take on the responsibility of raising their children. Being a responsible parent means providing your children with the skills necessary to become a successful and contributing citizen. It's impossible to be a good parent and a self-centred individual at the same time. By placing faith in the family structure the community benefits in a virtuous circle of reinforcing good habits.

None of this needs to be explicitly religious, but it should be noted that these communitarian ideals are an important part of living the Christian ethos on which our civilisation was founded. More explicit religious faith also acts as an instrument against downfall. Faith in an omniscient presence that guides our conscience and encourages our wellbeing is a great reminder that our thoughts, words and actions really do matter.

Some may take the cynical view that those who adhere to faith principles are simply wishing to avoid the negative consequences of their actions, both here and in the hereafter. Indeed this can be true. But what is wrong with avoiding the negative consequences which will follow intemperate behaviour? And what is wrong with being inclined to act virtuously because our conscience informs us so? Sometimes, that which we fear provides an effective deterrent to making poor choices; what we once referred to in a positive sense as 'taboos.' This too is an important aspect of our inherited traditions.

But fear is not at the heart of Christianity nor of our nation. The very essence of Christian faith lies in forgiveness. Christians believe that Jesus died so that we may live. He took upon himself our sins so that we may be forgiven and thereby gave us a model of forgiveness for others. This is a cycle that allows civility and progress in the face of man's faults and imperfectability.

It is arguably also a theological reason why the Christian West has developed a unique concept of human dignity as well as the legal and governmental structures necessary to create a society funded on individual liberty, voluntariness and personal responsibility. All of these concepts ultimately contribute to a civilisation capable of the scientific innovation and progress we can all benefit from today. It should not be forgotten that the intellectual foundations of the West, as it moved out of the Middle Ages, were inspired, not hindered, by Christianity and the institutions that gave it public and political expression. Sir Kenneth Clarke wrote:

> It could be argued that western civilisation was basically the creation of the Church. In saying that I am not thinking, for the moment, of the Church as a repository of Christian truth and spiritual experience: I am thinking of her as the twelfth century thought of her ... In so far as the intellectual and the emotional lives of men and women of the twelfth century rose above mere necessity, they were inspired and directed by the Church.[49]

The ideas that underpin our religious heritage are inseparable from the 'secular' values we can all enjoy today. Social engagement

---

49 Kenneth Clarke, *Civilisation* (British Broadcasting Corporation and John Murray, 1969) p. 35.

and inherited religious ethos are part of the same experience. As illustrated above, the communitarian spirit is a quintessentially conservative phenomenon, and the 'conservative revolutionary' should not shy away from affirming the unique cultural foundations of our community. Likewise, we should certainly not cower in the face of disingenuous attacks of the left on our religious traditions; traditions that the left would replace with abstract ideas completely divorced from human experience, ideas fundamentally incapable of addressing the deep problems that we all (religious and secular alike) face today.

These truths are far too often denied and derided by radicals and 'progressives' in popular culture, and this is why *we need a conservative revolution*.

## Faith and politics

Contrary to the constant mantra heard in the leftist and secular media, faith and politics go hand in hand. Politics is about people, the societies they form and how best to help them thrive. It's essentially about relationships. Politics seeks the best, the common good for all, and *this is a hallmark of Christian service*. Our laws are made in parliament, which is populated by politicians. It is not extraordinary that the law, which is inherently concerned with human relationships, will reflect the morality of the people, and *morality is a key religious concern*.

This, of course, should be nothing new. But today we live in such as hyper secular environment – where hostility to religion can be seen in the media on an almost daily basis, and especially to Christianity and its ethos – that propositions which were once obvious and needed no explanation or justification, now have to be re-asserted. Australian Catholic thinker and anti-Communist activist B.A. Santamaria put forward an eight point apologia for Christian involvement in the political process. It seems even more relevant today than it did in 1960:[50]

1. there are instances where political activity will affect religious interests and concerns;

2. when religious principles are at stake, its adherents have a legitimate reason to intervene in the political process;

3. the intervention must be effective as well as moral (i.e. it cannot be hypocritical) while its methods must be appropriate to changing political and social circumstances of the time (i.e. different political, social and economic situations will call on a different approach to effective and moral action);

4. the intervention will be either by way of individual action, or through voluntary associations;

5. the Code of Canon Law provides for such voluntary associations, however they remain separate entities from the Church itself (this point obviously concerns Catholic associations, but analogous principles may be relevant to other Christian associations who wish to participate in the political process as well);

6. existing 'organised interests' create a precedent by already making their presence felt through lobbying and activism within party structures (Santamaria here was referring to the Union movement and presumably by corollary, 'Big Business.' Today, we have a multitude of 'organised interests' all vying for influence);

7. there is no reason to argue that the only legitimately

50 Bartholomew A. Santamaria, 'Religion and Politics' *The Price of Freedom* (Campion, 1964) pp. 149-150. What follows is a summary of these propositions, with some additional comments for the sake of clarity and to illustrate the propositions' relevance today.

participating 'organised interests' within the political
process are to be economic (or to extend this proposition
today, secular);

8. society would be healthier politically if it freely and openly
   acknowledged the existence of 'organised interests' in
   the political process (and to extend this proposition,
   democratic society would be much healthier politically if
   it accepted that the much vaunted 'progressive' virtues of
   'openness', 'tolerance' and 'diversity' extended to being
   open to traditional concepts and Christian ethos, tolerating
   these and incorporating them as legitimate voices in the
   political forum).

Those who brandish the term 'separation of Church and State'
as a way of dismissing arguments for faith and morality in public life
and removing religion from the public square miss the point entirely.
The 'separation' so-called was initially a device to protect religious
institutions from interference by the state. This can be traced to the
Biblical injunction to render unto Caesar what is Caesar's and to
God what is God's,[51] as well as to St Augustine's discussion of the
relationship between the "heavenly society and the earthly city" in his
*City of God*, where he suggests that 'temporal things' should be treated
as 'supports' for Man's journey in life.[52]

Although those who enter politics assume a great duty – to be a
representative of the people and to always put their shared interest first
– asking our parliamentary representatives to dismiss their personal
belief structure is neither practical nor reasonable. However, acting
in the national interest means, whatever the religions persuasions of

---

51 Mt 22:21; Mk 12:17; Lk 20:25.
52 Aurelius Augustinus of Hippo (b. 354AD d. 430AD), *City of God* (written circa C.5th
first published 1467) bk. XIX ch. 17 (Penguin, 2003) pp. 877-879.

our representatives, that they need to maintain the foundations of our Christian heritage as the cornerstone of mainstream values. This is the case even where a majority of the electors may reject the morality on which the prosperity of their community depends. This is because true leadership is often defined by the willingness and ability to make difficult decisions, even if they are unpopular. Burke made this point in his famous speech to the electors of Bristol in 1774:

> Certainly, Gentlemen, it ought to be the happiness and glory of a representative to live in the strictest union, the closest correspondence, and the most unreserved communication with his constituents. Their wishes ought to have great weight with him; their opinions high respect; their business unremitted attention. It is his duty to sacrifice his response, his pleasure, his satisfactions, to theirs, – and above all, ever, and in all cases, to prefer their interest to his own.

> But his unbiased opinion, his mature judgment, his enlightened conscience, he ought not to sacrifice to you, to any man, or to any set of men living. These he does not derive from your pleasure, – no, nor from the law and the Constitution. They are a trust from Providence, for the abuse of which he is deeply answerable. Your representative owes you, not his industry only, but his judgment; and he betrays, instead of serving you, if he sacrifices it to your opinion.[53]

A country that is committed to values that have been tried and true is a country that can offer the most to its citizens. We have seen throughout history how catastrophic misguided leadership can be. Without a moral framework on which to base political decisions, it is easy for politicians of every stripe to choose the poorer course of action.

---

53 Edmund Burke, 'Speech at the Conclusion of the Poll in Bristol' (3 November 1774) as published in Robert Smith (ed) *Edmund Burke on Revolution* (Harper Touchbooks, 1986) p. 52.

Without faith in our fellow man and confidence in our political leaders, society will invariably suffer a crisis of trust. Ultimately, politics depends on our ability to persuade each other of common aims based on common reality. This depends on unity and a *sense of belonging* – the necessary preconditions of a democratic nation where both the religious and secular are heard, but where the values linking us all are perpetually strengthened.

As the process of globalisation continues apace, advances in communication and travel have potentially exposed our country to problems and threats we have never had to face before in our history. For example, individuals with access to the internet can now be exposed to exotic and hostile ideologies that may seem attractive to those who feel disconnected from their local communities or have violent objections to values on which our society was founded. Today we face unprecedented challenges. In addressing these, we cannot hope to entirely rid society of the potential for error. No religion or philosophy can assuage this.

The conservative accepts that even the best policy, the most successful economic management or the building of great communities cannot guarantee personal happiness. So too we will never be able to clear our nation of crime, or ensure that Australian society is at all times compassionate.

Hence we cannot rely on government alone to manage our moral responsibilities. A responsible citizenry and a strong culture is necessary instead. But what the government *can* do, is help to maintain and promote the conditions in which such a culture can grow and thrive. When this is achieved, the system will take care of itself through the voluntary activity of its constituents: individuals and associations all working together to create a healthy, prosperous society. Here we see the importance of voluntariness in this healthy, confident and therefore self-perpetuating system.

Our citizens deserve to know that human kindness is among the most abundant and precious of all qualities. But again, since our cultural framework informs us that virtue must be voluntary, kindness cannot be enforced through state action the way the radical would have it (such as, through high taxation and welfare). The citizen can only understand and feel the drive to contribute to society when he has had the opportunity to demonstrate and be a recipient of this initiative himself. Australians most certainly need faith in their politicians and system of government but most importantly, they must have faith in themselves. In exercising his own conscience and judgment, the conservative politician should take a principled stance on public policy and ensure that the necessary groundwork is laid on which such a community can develop.

From time to time, some have been tempted to believe that society has become too complex to be managed by self-rule and that government by an elite group is superior to government for, by and of the people. But this path of least resistance is rarely, if ever, the better way; for if no one among us is capable of governing themselves, who among us has the capacity to govern someone else?

As reflected in Kirk's first principles of the conservative, despite all manner of ideological hope, there is no perfect society. A system based on personal choice brings us closest to such ideals. However, freedom of choice brings with it moral dilemmas, as well as a need for self-discipline and responsibility. Here again we see the importance of a moral framework in which liberty can be enjoyed, and outside of which freedom is an illusion.

We must continue to strive for these qualities to be restored among the Australian community. While we cannot build a utopian society, we can nevertheless shape one that is strong, cohesive and prosperous.

We must continue to aim for this: an Australia built around personal qualities of industry, honesty, responsibility and justice.

Realising this ambition requires an Australia led by purpose and ethic; an Australia that reflects the cultural legacy in which self-reliance is a primary concern, and where this self-reliance is couched in the moral and ethical framework essential for a competent national government. The only political tendency which is capable of delivering this is one that respects and affirms tradition. This is why *we need a conservative revolution*.

## The threat to faith

Faith and observance of the religious tradition, without which our civilisation would simply not exist, are under threat. A number of those threats have already been raised earlier in this chapter. These include the failure to pass on critical values to our children and the rise of a new environmentalism that displays the hallmarks of a cultish and intolerant neo-paganism.

Indeed the greatest threats to faith manifest themselves in attacks on Christianity in particular. These are worrying to the conservative, not simply because our traditional social mores are being challenged but because religion, with few exceptions, has been and remains a key element of conservative thought.

Conservatism has been largely based on a Christian worldview. Burke recognised religion as the base of a "civil society" and Christianity as "one great source of civilisation."[54] Likewise, Lord Hugh Cecil in his tome *Conservatism* (1912) wrote:

> The championship of religion is therefore the most important
> of the functions of Conservatism. It is the keystone of

---

54 Edmund Burke, *op cit.*, p. 188.

the arch upon which the whole fabric rests. As long as Conservatism makes the fulfilment of its duties to religion the first of its purposes, it will be saved from the two principal dangers that alternatively threaten it: the danger of sinking into a mere factious variation of Liberalism, supporting the claims of another set of politicians, but propounding measures not distinguished by any pervading principle: or the other danger of standing only for the defence of those who are well off, without any sincere endeavour to consider the interests of the whole people, or any higher object than the triumph of the sagacious selfishness of the prosperous.[55]

In explicitly identifying conservatism with Christianity, Burke and those who were inspired by his insights provide a powerful platform for the rejection of other religious agendas that compromise or threaten to undermine our traditional values. It should not, however, be misunderstood that traditionalist conservatism is based on a 'rejectionist' attitude; instead, what Burke and his followers were doing was simply affirming the rights of their cultural heritage within its political order. Furthermore, it is not just conservative philosophers who see our particular religious tradition as a cornerstone of conservatism.

Pope Pius XI discussed the Christian principle of 'subsidiarity' in his encyclical *Quadragesimo Anno* (1931) when he wrote:

Just as it is gravely wrong to take from individuals what they can accomplish by their own initiative and industry and give it to the community, so also it is an injustice … to assign to a greater or higher association what lesser or subordinate organisations can do.[56]

This reflects how the conservative suspicion of all forms

---

55 Hugh Richard Heathcote Cecil, *Conservatism* (Williams and Noregate, 1912) pp. 116-117.
56 Pius XI, *Quadragesimo Anno* (15 May 1931) § 79. See also earlier reference to the work of John Horvat II, *op. cit.*

of levelling, the reduction of everything to its lowest common denominator of bland sameness (which usually follows 'progressive' programs) and the conservative restraint against the abuse of power are both consistent with Christian teaching and values.

Today, there are two such competing political and religious ideologies that threaten to undermine our Western culture. One involves the collectivist message of Marxism while the other represents a dark totalitarian agenda inherent to fundamentalist religion.

### *The green agenda*

The first of these comes via the so-called 'green movement.' In seeking to close down human industry, the green agenda has the demise of Western culture and implicitly the Christian values at its core. According to green philosophy, the plant is equal to an animal and that animal is equal to man. Thus mankind has been relegated to just another species amongst species in the green priority list. This is a repudiation of the principle of *Imago Dei* and therefore vacates our understanding of human dignity to the extremely dangerous pseudo-rationalisations of militant secularists. As illustrated earlier in this book, we are already starting to witness the fruit of some of these disturbing trends in social policy and law.

Ironically, and perhaps hypocritically, the radical green agenda regards human beings as being a "cancer on nature"[57] yet affords monkeys and orangutans 'human rights' that they would deny their fellow man.[58] By these standards, the great apes have a right to life

---

57 This assertion is attributed to David Foreman, the founder of 'Earth First!' a radical environmentalist movement based in the United States. As quoted in Michael Pollen, 'Only Man's Presence Can Save Nature: Beyond the Wilderness, *Harper's Magazine*, vol 280, issue 1679 (April 1990), p. 48.

58 Peter Singer co-founded the Great Ape Project in 1993 with the aim of giving certain rights to great apes such as the right to life and the right to liberty.

but the unborn and infirm have no such privilege. Such claims defy common sense and undermine the natural law that is written on all our hearts. Disappointingly, this has not stopped such beliefs from achieving a level of legitimacy which simply cannot be justified by any moral criterion.

In placing an inverse relationship to the natural order, this green zealotry (for this is what it has become) has displaced the enduring values illustrated by our traditional moral beliefs. Those conservative beliefs which have withstood the tests of time and provided the bedrock for a spiritually rich and intellectually wealthy civilisation to flourish in the West are now being replaced by a soulless and hostile cultural Marxism hidden under a green skin.

Their misplaced values extend to denying, on spurious environmental grounds, the development of base load energy systems required to power their lifestyle. Most recently this has been the 'global warming' or 'climate change' movement that has developed a cult-like following among the political left. Seemingly oblivious to the natural weather fluctuations and change our world has been experiencing for millennia, the global warming alarmists blame Man for every new climate event.

All 'good thinking' citizens are now supposed to believe a heatwave is a product of 'global warming' while a cold snap is due to 'climate change.' Cyclonic activity, unusual rainfall and drought are all allegedly caused by Man-made carbon dioxide. If only we could all stop respiring we would be sure to save the planet!

The green solution is not just to limit industry and activity that has sustained the development of our wealth and progress, but to remove choice, autonomy and self-determination from the people and deliver all important decision-making processes to government.

All of this is proposed as a solution to a problem which is still hotly debated between scientists and professionals, many of whom even question whether there is a problem at all. Those scientists and investigators who dissent from the 'consensus' are defamed and ridiculed. But a responsible government policy would never ignore the work of Robert Carter[59] or Ian Plimer,[60] nor would it ignore the warnings of Václav Klaus,[61] Bjørn Lomborg,[62] Roy Spencer[63] or Lord Monckton of Brenchley.[64] They all raise legitimate concerns, yet for all the alleged open-mindedness of 'progressives', they are never treated with the seriousness they deserve.

### Islam and 'international Jihad'

Similarly we have the increasing indulgence of a totalitarian political agenda in the guise of the religion of Islam. The fact that the Islamic political and religious ideology is incompatible with Western culture has been demonstrated throughout history. Churchill wrote in *The River War* (1899):

> No stronger retrograde force exists in the world. Far from being moribund, Mohammedanism is a militant and proselytising faith. It has already spread throughout Central Africa, raising fearless warriors at every step; and were it not that Christianity is sheltered in the strong arms of

---

59 Robert Carter, *Climate: The Counter Consensus* (Stacey International, 2010).

60 Ian Plimer, *Heaven + Earth – Global Warming: The Missing Science* (Connor Court, 2009).

61 Václav Klaus, *Blue Planet in Green Shackles – What is Endangered: Climate or Freedom?* (Competitive Enterprise Institute, 2008).

62 Bjørn Lomborg, *Cool It – The Skeptical Environmentalist's Guide to Global Warming* (Marshall Cavendish, 2007).

63 Roy Spencer, *Climate Confusion – How Global Warming Hysteria Leads to Bad Science, Pandering Politicians and Misguided Policies that Hurt the Poor* (Encounter, 2008).

64 Christopher Monckton, 'Climategate: Caught Green-Handed', *Science and Public Policy Institute Occasional Paper* (7 December 2009).

science – the science against which it had vainly struggled – the civilisation of modern Europe might fall, as fell the civilisation of ancient Rome.[65]

Brilliant a political leader that Churchill was, this was no original insight. In 1835, Alexis de Tocqueville reflected in his *Democracy in America*:

> Muhammad brought down from heaven and put into the Koran not religious doctrines only, but political maxims, criminal and civil laws, and scientific theories. The Gospels on the other hand, deal only with the general relations between man and God and between man and man. Beyond that, they teach nothing and do not oblige people to believe anything. That alone, among a thousand reasons, is enough to show that Islam will not be able to hold its power long in ages of enlightenment and democracy, while Christianity is destined to reign in such ages, as in all others.[66]

It seems that with the embrace of a secular equality devoid of moral grounding, most of our political elite now find it impossible to draw what were once obvious qualitative distinctions between religious world-views and philosophies of life. No doubt this is the result of people's desire to avoid bigotry and 'discrimination', but what it has actually achieved is an impoverished political debate. Instead of being 'enlightened', political discourse has in fact become less able to tackle uncomfortable truths.

Tocqueville and Churchill had reason to make their observations about the nature of Islam, so many decades ago, but these reasons are with us today. It does say quite a great deal about the poor state

---

65 Winston Churchill, *The River War – An Historical Account of the Reconquest of the Soudan* (Longmans Green & Co., 1899) vol. 2 pp. 249-250.

66 Alexis de Tocqueville, *Democracy in America* vol. 2, pt. 2, ch. 5 (Harper Perennial Classics edition, 2006) p. 445.

of contemporary political leadership when merely acknowledging the obvious is considered 'controversial' or a sign of bad character.

Earlier I recounted Cardinal Pell's comment that our Western concept of human dignity is necessarily derived from our uniquely Christian cultural heritage. Pell made this observation by contrasting it with Islam:

> It is frequently observed today in relation to events in the Arab world that democracy is not something that can be imposed; that democracy needs a certain sort of culture to make it possible. For the West, that culture is fundamentally Christian.[67]

In considering Islam, it is important for conservatives to separate the edicts of Islam from the practice of many so-called 'secular' Muslims. These are the many Muslims who practise the spiritual aspects of their personal faith or adhere to daily customs in their life routines, but do not necessarily follow the teachings of the trilogy of Islamic texts (*Quran*, *Hadith* and *Sira*) which are dominated by matters perhaps better described as *political*, not *spiritual*.[68] Often these are people who are Muslim by cultural practice and tradition rather than through strong religious belief. In considering these people as 'moderate Muslims', one must recognise that there is no such thing as moderate Islam because the Islamic doctrines are very clear.[69]

---

67 George Pell, *op cit.*, p. 53.

68 The *Sira* is Mohammad's biography, the *Hadith* are the reported traditions of Mohammad and the *Quran* is a book Muslims believe represents what was received by Mohammad through allegedly divine revelation. This is the smallest part of the Islamic doctrine.

69 For example, Somali-born writer, activist and former politician Ayaan Hirsi Ali grew up as a Muslim but has since become an outspoken critic of Islam. Hirsi Ali has been reported as saying "I don't believe there is such a thing as 'moderate Islam'": Mary Wakefield, "We are at war with all Islam': An interview with Ayaan Hirsi Ali', *The Spectator* (online) (28 November 2007) <www.spectator.co.uk> (accessed 21 July 2013). Print edition not available to the writer.

This is apparent not only from the demands of the Islamic tradition itself, particularly in light of the absence from its worldview of any separation of religion and state, but also according to the pronouncements of modern Islamic political leaders. For example, the Prime Minister of Turkey, Recep Tayyip Erdoğan, forthrightly rejected the concept of a 'moderate Islam.' In August of 2007 he bluntly said:

> These descriptions are very ugly, it is offensive and an insult
> to our religion. There is no moderate or immoderate Islam.
> Islam is Islam and that's it.[70]

These are not the words of an 'Islamophobe', they are the words of a Muslim head of state of a secular country where over 99 per cent of the population identify as Muslim.[71] The Islamic doctrine commands Muslims to establish *Sharia* (or Islamic law) wherever Muslims settle in significant populations. The *Sharia*, based upon the *Quran, Sira* and *Hadith* (which are oral and recorded traditions used to interpret the *Sharia*), forms a code which dictates the life routines of its adherents to the smallest detail, even which hand a Muslim should use when greeting a 'non-believer.' Ultimately, it commands Muslims to impose Islam on the entire world and to use *jihad* (or holy war) in their quest for political domination.

Islam and the *Quran* are a blueprint for an ideology that seeks to create an Islamic super-state and dominate every detail of life in an Islamic society. It rules over what to eat and how to dress. Adulterers are to be stoned to death and homosexuals punished. Women are

---

70 MEMRI blog entry, 'PM Erdogan: the terms Moderate Islam is ugly and offensive; there is no Moderate Islam; Islam is Islam' Middle East Media Research Institute (undated) <www.memriblog.org/turkey> (accessed 9 June 2013); this information was originally sourced by MEMRI from Milliyet Turkey of 21 August 2007.

71 United States Library of Congress, Federal Research Division, 'Country Profile: Turkey' (2008) <www.loc.gov/index.html> (accessed 19 July 2013) p. 10.

considered second class citizens. Non-believers are excluded from full membership of society and those who commit apostasy can be killed.[72]

In his book *Islam and the Jews*, former lecturer of Islamic history at Egypt's Al-Azhar University, Dr. Mark Gabriel, himself a convert to Christianity, explained Muslim protestations that Islam is the religion of peace. According to Gabriel such claims can only be explained in one of two ways:

1. Wishful thinking [the devout Muslim] really believes that Islam should be about peace so he preaches the peaceful side of Islam. He sincerely believes he is practicing Islam, but peace is not the final revelation of Islam.

2. Deception ... in Islam a Muslim may profess to deny nasikh [i.e., the abrogation of Sharia] if doing so is for the purpose of protecting the image of Islam and furthering missionary activity. This is particularly acceptable if the Muslim is living as a minority in a non-Muslim country ... But this denial must be in words only. In their hearts, Muslims must continue to accept nasikh and follow the full and final development of the Quranic revelation.[73]

This may seem like an unnecessarily blunt assessment, but based solely on its own dictates and teachings, and judging by the recent history of its followers in the West since the terrorist attacks in New York, London, Madrid and against Australians in Bali in 2002, as well as the practices of its fundamentalist adherents in the major capitals of Western Europe, Islamic law does not seem to be particularly compatible with the values on which our society has been founded.

---

72 For further discussion on some of these elements, see Mark Durie, *The Third Choice: Islam, Dhimmitude and Freedom* (Deror, 2010).

73 Mark A. Gabriel, *Islam and the Jews* (Front Line, 2003) p. 53.

This has been legally affirmed by the European Court of Human Rights which ruled in 2001 that "[i]t is difficult to declare one's respect for democracy and human rights while at the same time supporting a regime based on sharia".[74]

A steadily growing body of recent literature, specifically addressing this problem as it is experienced in Europe, provides an insight to what we may expect here unless these issues are honestly and thoughtfully confronted by responsible policy. Likewise, a truly responsible government would be foolish to ignore the warnings of Ed Hussein,[75] Christopher Caldwell,[76] Melanie Phillips,[77] Geert Wilders[78] and the many others who continue to write about the Islamic reality experienced in the cities and streets where they live. In his 2006 book *Girls Like You* Paul Sheehan illustrates that such concerns are not unfounded even for us in Australia.[79] Ironically, it is the 'progressives' who should really be up in arms, as it is their radical 'freedoms' which will be the first to go if Sharia is ever practised in Western societies. Mark Steyn humorously writes in the prologue to his 2006 book *America Alone*:

> [L]efties always respond "Oh, well, that's typical right-wing racism." In fact, it ought to be the Left's issue. I'm a "social conservative." When the Mullahs take over, I'll grow my beard a little fuller, get a couple extra wives, and keep my head down. It's the feminists and gays who'll have a tougher time.[80]

---

74 *Refah Partisi (The Welfare Party) and Others v Turkey* (2001) Eur Court HR Application nos. 41340/98, 41342/98, 41343/98 and 41344/98.

75 Ed Hussein, *The Islamist* (Penguin, 2007).

76 Christopher Caldwell, *Reflections on the Revolution in Europe* (Penguin, 2009).

77 Melanie Phillips, *Londonistan* (rev. ed. by Gibson Square, 2008).

78 Geert Wilders, *Marked for Death* (Regnery, 2012).

79 Paul Sheehan, *Girls Like You* (Macmillan, 2006).

80 Mark Steyn, *America Alone* (Regnery, 2006) p. xxvii.

One may disagree with the following proposition, but an argument can certainly be made that Islam is a threat to our faith and our culture because it seeks to dominate and change the founding values of our society with those that are incompatible with the Western way of life: it has a concept of human dignity which is fundamentally different from ours, it does not recognise the separation of church and state nor the equality of men and women. The idea of freedom of speech and freedom of religion under Islamic rule is also vastly at odds with what we understand by those freedoms. And of course, it is no friend to 'progressive' social programs. The left often talks about the need to 'celebrate diversity' and how it can apparently enrich society, but not all differences are worthy of celebration because not all cultural values are compatible with ours, nor are all differences 'good' in the sense that they are beneficial to us.

The differences between the Christian and the Islamic worldviews are too radical to simply ignore. Unfortunately, they are ignored all too often, probably because our political leaders don't understand the importance of affirming the primacy of our own culture, and at the same time, they seek approval from cultural and moral relativists among the left. This is why *we need a conservative revolution.*

## Faith in Australia and its people

Although the threats to our traditional faith and values are ever present, we should still have faith in the future. Conservatism is not backward looking. It respects the past and looks towards the future. There is good reason for us to have faith in Australia and her people. We have faced adversity before and demonstrated our capacity to meet all challenges that history has provided us.

However, we will only be able to respond to the serious erosion of the values that have proven themselves since time immemorial, into the brave new world of moral relativism, moral vacuums and brutal theocracy if we can restore the spiritual and moral traditions as the core of our democracy.

That will require the overturning of the new orthodoxy where 'anything goes' and the continuing indulgence of personal appetites. This will require conservative Australians to speak out against the decline in our social graces and moral framework that both faith and the respect for our moral heritage provide.

However, speaking *against* things is not the recipe for success in seeking to restore the strength of the conservative pillars in our nation. The conservative revolution will require good men and women to speak *in favour of* the guiding principles that have demonstrated their enduring value over previous generations. By speaking up for the things that matter we can lift society up to make it better. That is the essence of the conservative revolution.

It is time to stop being defensive in our attitude to politics. Too much damage has been done by the so-called 'progressives' for a compromised approach to cultural and national renewal to succeed today. The values and ideas we stand for are not things to be ashamed of; they are the solid building blocks of our communities and civilisation. One day, we will have to answer to our children who will face the consequence of radical social, economic and political experiments. Where were we when we could have stopped the rot and made a difference, they will undoubtedly ask.

We simply do not have the right not to argue our case, fearlessly and with confidence in the truth of our position. This is why *we need a conservative revolution*.

# 3

# The Second Pillar: Family

There is no guidebook for life, no clear path through it. Our family is often the best model we have. It shapes the attitudes, the hopes, the ambitions and the values of the child more than any other force.

Unless we work to strengthen the family, to create conditions under which parents can do their best and where families can prosper, everything else – schools and playgrounds, public assistance and private concern – will be of little lasting value.

The lessons learned in the home – ones of patience, encouragement, tolerance, reciprocity, the values and importance of faith – are carried by children into adulthood. In tandem, I believe it is vital for our young people to understand the role that goodwill and community service play in their nation's success.

The ideal way for this to occur is through both observation and participation. When parents set an example of compassion and extend a hand to the less fortunate, their children will feel compelled to do the same.

As children experience their parents' love and care, they come to understand what it is to be part of a strong family, a strong community and a strong society.

Without the strength and example of families in our community, entire societies can suffer. When families collapse it is usually the children who are damaged. When this happens on a large scale, the very basis of society is under threat.

## Family as the foundation of society

The family is at the very foundation of our society. It is the primary building block in which we learn to love and be loved, where we learn to share and to compromise. It seems trite to have to state this, but evidently social planners need to be reminded that the family is the first institution where three fundamental lessons are learned by each individual: a healthy and fulfilling relationship between the genders, respect for authority, and cooperation in working together as a larger whole. Interfering with this will mean interfering with the first school in which good citizenship is taught to the next generation.

The family allows us to learn from our mistakes without lasting judgment or recrimination. We learn to balance our personal needs against the needs of others and the broader interests of our closest relatives. Families teach patience and understanding, and share life's best and worst moments with us.

Our social behaviour is shaped within our families and they are the best means of passing on critical values to the next generation. In families we first learn the natural limits of personal expression. Families also draw us together as individuals. No matter how disparate our interests or personalities or geography, we all have one thing in common – we were created through the unity of male and female, and thus all have a mother and father. In a world where technology threatens to supersede the need for a man and woman to be involved in the creation of life, the importance of family takes on new meaning.

It also raises the question about what price is ultimately attached to the creation of life outside of the familial norm. While the social sciences will only be able to measure the real cost after a generation or more of research, we can make reasonable predictions based upon the norm (having a mother and father and being raised in their care) and the known effects of a child being raised in sub-optimal circumstances. The risks are significant yet the benefits, while often very personal, are definitely limited. What is missing in the push for human cloning, *in vitro* fertilisation and surrogacy, for example, is the understanding that children come into families as gifts, not commodities and not trophies. Being able to understand this important distinction in attitude towards new life requires the traditional understanding of human dignity which is part of our religious heritage, as described earlier in the First Pillar.

Evidence (i.e., not religious dictates) supports the notion that children raised in strong and traditionally structured families go on to be more successful in key measures, while also making a strong contribution to the strength of their communities. Families teach us something that some civil libertarians rather we'd forget. Namely, that the rights of the individual are not only shaped by the context of the family. They are also properly limited by the family in ways that allow freedom of expression and personal choice, while also respecting the rights and freedoms of other family members and the overarching responsibilities to the family as an entity in its own right.

## Importance of traditional marriage

The role of marriage in creating a strong family unit should not be underestimated. As David Blankenhorn pointed out in *The Future of Marriage* (2007) marriage is not just a private relationship, it is a public institution. Blankenhorn wrote:

> Social institutions exist to meet basic human needs. An institution that exists everywhere on the planet, in addition to whatever else it may be doing in this or that specific locale, is also obviously meeting at least one primary, cross-cultural human need. Regarding marriage, we have not identified

that need. If human beings were not sexually embodied creatures who everywhere reproduce sexually and give birth to helpless, socially needy offspring who remain immature for long periods of time and who therefore depend on the love and support of *both of the parents who brought them into existence, the world almost certainly would not include the institution of marriage.*[81]

At its heart, marriage remains a bond between a man and woman, both of whom love each other and consider joining their individual lives into a permanent union that will provide the best opportunity to achieve their hopes and dreams, and provide the best possible environment for the raising of children. Combining their fates through marriage represents the most intimate and profound moral investment they can make for the future not only of their family, but to their country as well: no children means no future, especially for a people who believe that they are living for something more than mere self-gratification. To raise the next generation is one of the most valuable contributions to the preservation of our culture that any married couple can make.

Of course, there are many benefits afforded through traditional marriage, some codified by the state and others a product of centuries of observation as well as ongoing empirical studies. It is not necessary to recount a list of these findings here, but what is clear is that the conservative argument for traditional social policy is not without strong merits. However, one recent report can be singled out for specific attention because it proves that women living in traditional marriage structures report higher levels of satisfaction and happiness. A study by Bradford Wilcox and Steven Nock, both of Virginia University, found that adhering to traditional norms create incentives

---

81 David Blankenhorn, *The Future of Marriage* (Encounter, 2009) p. 102.

for husbands and wives to work at the marriage. The result is a mutually beneficial and satisfactory arrangement.[82]

Moreover, virtually every reputable analysis of morbidity by marital status shows that married people tend to live longer than divorced or single people. These findings are confirmed across countries and cultures through myriad of studies conducted since the 1930s.[83] This also suggests that married people are healthier and this claim is supported by empirical studies into marriage and health. Such studies find that married people are less likely to experience mental health problems, be victims of suicide or consume high levels of alcohol and other drugs.

Married people also tend to be wealthier than the non-married. At one level this may be counter intuitive given than married people often have the additional expense of raising children. It could also be explained away by the fact a married couple where both are employed do not have twice the expenses of a single person. However, a 2001 study by Donna Gunther and Madeline Zavodny published in the *Journal of Population Economics* showed that married men actually earn around 15 per cent more than their non-married counterparts.[84] Once again, the conclusion may indeed be counter-intuitive: one might think the single person would have more time to devote to their work than those with important external commitments. However, reality suggests that when an individual has the support of a wife or husband

82 Bradford Wilcox and Steven Nock, 'What's Love Got To Do With It? Equality, Equity, Commitment and Women's Marital Quality' *Social Forces* (November, 2006) vol. 84 no. 3 pp. 1339-1342 [doi: 10.1353/sof.2006.0076].
83 For a summary of studies about the benefits of marriage, see *21 Reasons Why Marriage Matters* (2nd ed., Fatherhood Foundation, 2009)
84 Dina K. Gunther and Madeline Zavodny, 'Is the Male Marriage Premium Due to Selection? The Effect of Shotgun Weddings on the Return to Marriage' *J Popul Econ* (June 2011) vol. 14 no. 2 [doi:10.1007/s001480000058].

and a stable home life, they tend to be more productive at work. This important stability of home life is also stronger in married couples than in other forms of relationships. David Blankenhorn found that:

> scholarly research now shows that participating in the institution of marriage – being subject to its rules and incentives and being guided by it public meaning – adds stability and longevity to a relationship. After all, that's one of the main purposes of the institution.[85]

But marriage is far more than a benefit to the individual. Society as a whole benefits from the relationship in a variety of ways, perhaps none as important and immediately practical as the maintenance of our population through the bearing of healthy and well-adjusted children. That's why the state has always protected and advantaged marriage, the one existing institution that everyone can participate in which predates the state itself.

Put simply, married couples tend to be more likely to have children than those in other types of relationships. In fact, they are more than twice as likely to have children as those of the same age in de facto relationships. Those children they do have are more likely to be emotionally and psychologically centred than children who have grown up in other familial structures.[86]

The need to procreate and sustain our population is one very important benefit to society that is supported through traditional marriage. The benefits to society through marriage are recognised

---

85 David Blankenhorn, *op cit.*, p. 145.

86 For a summary of studies about the benefits of marriage for children, see *21 Reasons Why Marriage Matters* (2nd ed., Fatherhood Foundation, 2009). Also see Sarah Wise, 'Family Structure, child outcomes and environmental mediators: An overview of the Development in Diverse Families study', *Australian Institute of Family Studies Research Paper* No. 30 (January 2003) pp. 5-6.

and so society, in turn, should provide benefits to people who are married. A radical may mischievously reply that people don't have to marry to have and raise children. On the face of it this is true, but it is a disingenuous retort. Science itself supports the contention that traditional marriage provides the best environment in which a *functional* citizenry of the future can be mentored. Not for nothing the opening passages of Daniel Amneus' 1990 book *The Garbage Generation* state that an overwhelming majority of those who end up being processed through the criminal justice system come from broken families (or what 'progressives' like to euphemistically call 'alternative family models').[87] It is perfectly reasonable and rational therefore for the state, if it *is* to have a role in social policy and the affairs of marriage, to *reinforce and entrench those aspects of traditional marriage that work*, not undermine them and promote 'alternatives' which have led to social chaos.

While discussing the benefits of marriage, it is also apparent that there are many reasons to support marriage other than those related to children. The radical may well say, that if married people are healthier and wealthier, surely society should be encouraging more people to get married, including those who are in same-sex relationships. To support that conclusion is to ignore the evidence supporting the traditional family unit and the important roles of the mother and father as unique participants in the development of their children. There are other benefits, yes, but they are intrinsically and inexorably linked to the first and primary good of marriage: the family unit.

---

87 Daniel Amneus, *The Garbage Generation* (Primrose Press, 1990). Amneus refers to the work of Ramsey Clarke, *Crime in America: Observations on its Nature, Causes, Prevention and Control* (Poke Books, 1970). These common sense notions are obvious to the conservative, but rejected by the radical even if studies have proven their relevance for decades.

## The traditional family unit

Today's families don't always fit the traditional archetype. Many children are raised by a single parent. Others have grandparents as primary caregivers. Some households include members of the extended family while others have little or no external familial support.

In a society where advocacy for the ideal is often derided as unrealistic and anachronistic, and given the increasing number of 'non-traditional' families, there is a temptation to equate all family structures as being equal or relative. Indeed, there are those who advocate that 'non-traditional' families (including same-sex couples) are actually better for children than having a mother and father who love each other and live together in traditional marriage![88]

The Fatherhood Foundation, in their *21 Reasons Why Gender Matters* (2007) state that "the natural family, cemented by marriage, is a mini welfare state, education system, health care service and socialising institution."[89] This statement encapsulates the importance of the traditional family as the ideal environment in which to raise children. Simon Berger, himself a homosexual, articulated his opposition to 'gay marriage' in Australia's short-lived *Conservative* magazine in February, 2006. His sober observations are worth repeating here:

> When I was first exposed to the gay community, I couldn't help but notice for example, the preponderance of sex venues and the rarity of long term, monogamous relationships and wonder why so many gay men's lives seemed to revolve

---

88 Simon Crouch, Elizabeth Waters, Ruth McNair, Jennifer Power and Elise Davis, 'Australian study of child health in same-sex families: background research, design and methodology' *BMC Public Health (2012)* vol. 12 no. 646 [doi:10.1186/1471-2458-12-646].
89 Various authors, *21 Reasons Why Gender Matters* (Fatherhood Foundation, 2007) §8 'Gender complementarity in a life-long marriage between a man and a woman is needed for a healthy, stable society' p. 9. In support of this contention, the Fatherhood Foundation also refers to Maggie Gallagher, *The Abolition of Marriage* (Regnery Publishing, 1996).

around sex ... Is there a cultural factor – that when an entire community is defined by sex, the preoccupation becomes self-perpetuating?

If you subscribe to the biology theory, this could reinforce the argument that changing the institutions of marriage and family means tampering with forces we don't fully understand. If you subscribe to the "if it feels good, do it" cultural theory (which would also explain the disproportionately rampant drug use) the promotion of this culture through events such as the Mardi Gras could contradict gay activists' claims to equal qualification for the responsibility of nurturing the next generation.

Personally, my decision not to have kids is based on a more simple view, predicated on nothing more than my personal experience: I'd want my kids to have a mum.

While these theories and my personal choice are not beyond refute, the "conservative" in me nonetheless believes that the family is too important an institution for governments to tinker with and too important a cultural foundation for government to undermine.[90]

Simon Berger's argument is rational, reasoned and lucid. In today's sensationalist environment, where almost all opposition to 'progressive' policy is treated as some kind of personal affront, Berger's level-headed reflections are rare. Men of reason should be thankful for his courage in 'coming out' as a policy analyst who is not swayed by his personal inclinations. He provides evidence that a conservative can oppose the radical policy initiatives that redefine ancient institutions without having to be motivated by malice or 'hate'.

---

90 Simon Berger, 'Coming Out as a Conservative Liberal' *Conservative* no. 2 (February 2006) pp. 22-23.

Unfortunately, we cannot expect this honesty from all quarters. There is a growing body of 'advocacy research' (which often starts from preconceived conclusions and works backwards, dressing itself in the rhetoric of science and impartiality) that seeks to 'prove' what we know intuitively and through direct, personal experience, to be false. Notwithstanding such 'studies', in general terms it is clear that married heterosexual parents are the best role models for children and that there is a great importance attached to bringing up children in a family with married parents. Put simply, having both parents around to support, guide and share with children is in the best interests of the child. Clearly fathers are the best people to teach their sons about manhood through both example and instruction. Similarly, the lessons passed on from mother to daughter cannot be easily (if at all) replicated outside of the familial environment.

Again, the radical will respond that in a same-sex 'marriage' a child will still be able to obtain the necessary instruction from close family friends or neighbours of the lacking sex. Why then the levels of criminality among boys and promiscuity among girls who are brought up in single parent families, more often than not headed by a single mother?[91] Are we to assume that these poor children have never met a member of their opposite gender, or had close family friends or neighbours of the opposite gender who could influence them and their social development? Perhaps it should be noted here too that in precisely this 'alternative' family environment, a child will be exposed

---

91 Even Barack Obama recognised the impact of fatherlessness on society when he said in 2008: "We know the statistics – that children who grow up without a father are five times more likely to live in poverty and commit crime; nine times more likely to drop out of schools and twenty times more likely to end up in prison. They are more likely to have behavioural problems, or run away from home, or become teenage parents themselves. And the foundations of our community are weaker because of it." 'Obama's Father's Day remarks', *New York Times* (online) (15 June 2008) <www.nytimes.com> (accessed 21 July 2013). Print edition not available to writer.

to a far greater risk of abuse than he or she would be if raised in a traditional environment.

So, in an attempt to liberate society from the oppression of allegedly 'arcane' or 'irrelevant' ideas about marriage, the social reformer will deliver children into a potentially dysfunctional environment which is far more dangerous to their emotional, psychological and physical development. And to compound the absurdity, these people call themselves 'progressives'. For all their alleged reason and rationality, for all their appeals to science, for all their mindless talk of 'equality' the radical is chronically impoverished by rejecting the inherent wisdom of tradition.

The extent of the damage done by the social revolution of the 1960s can be measured by the need to have to explain the obvious today. When did it become necessary to explain that the process of having gender-specific role models, strengthened by the security of marriage and unconditional love, enables the natural progression of life skills from father to son and mother to daughter? Similarly, the relationship between mother and son, father and daughter is vital for the full development of children into balanced and responsible adults and for an appropriate development in understanding their sexuality as they develop into adulthood.

Thus, contrary to what some radicals would have you believe, each parent has specific and unique roles directly related to gender. It is important to accept that there are differences between men and women and that by acknowledging these differences in no way implies superiority of one over another. Put simply, men and women are equal, but different. Those differences are complementary and together they work for the betterment of society, primarily through the raising of children.

By bringing different gifts to the role of parenthood, men and women support the complete development of the child. It is important for society to protect, foster and support the concept of complementary parenting as the ideal that should form the mainstay of our families, instead of undermining the distinct and valuable role played by men and women, as men and women. In doing so, we accept the responsibilities that parents have in raising children and the unique roles that gender plays in their development.

Historically the male role has been seen to be one of protector and breadwinner. In many instances they have also served as the authority figure within a household. This is not 'oppression,' it is a core responsibility. These roles can be traced back to our ancient ancestors where men undertook the hazardous hunting of game to provide sustenance to the tribe. Without food the family would die and authority was automatically attached to the successful hunter as he earned the respect of his community. Such specialised roles were common across different cultures and nations and in many instances continue today, albeit in very different circumstances.

Similarly, all cultures undertook that sons were trained by male role models in the skills that were required of manhood. In more modern times the role of the father continues to be as a guide for his children, especially to guide their sons in the ways of being a man, being a father, and the responsibilities that come with those roles.

This responsibility continues today. Men have a different relationship with their children (particularly sons) than do women. Play between fathers and sons is generally more robust and competitive, their games more aggressive, often revolving around physical prowess.

There is a strength and value that comes with this male heritage, a strength and value that benefits society even today. Although the particular tasks undertaken by men have changed over the centuries and millennia, all communities benefit from having uniquely male qualities which can be called upon when the circumstances require it. This male heritage contributes to a sense of identity among men. We can see how undermining this identity among young men today leads to a distorted, caricaturised, poorly developed and misguided sense of manhood. Strong, centred men will create strong and stable societies; the alternative is the moral chaos we see around us today.

Mothers too have specific roles in relation to children, the most obvious evidenced by the fact that they carry and bear children. They bond with children through the early acts of physical intimacy which only mothers can offer and are of lasting benefit to children, strengthening their health and wellbeing. Throughout their lives, women use their greater verbal ability to assist them in raising children and teaching them many important life lessons. Instinctively, most mothers recognise the special relationship they have with their children and its importance to their overall wellbeing and development. One nationwide study by the Institute of American Values reported that 93 per cent of mothers surveyed agreed that a "mother's contribution to the care of her children is so unique that no one else can replace it."[92]

The distinct but complementary roles of a mother and father in raising children are most notable when examining the consequences of their absence. Echoing the work of Ramsey Clarke and Daniel Amneus in 1970 and 1990 respectively, social commentator Bill Muehlenberg also noted that a study of British communities found a strong statistical link "between single parenthood and virtually every

---

92 Martha Erickson and Enola Aird, *The Motherhood Study – Fresh Insights on Mothers' Attitudes and Concerns* (Institute of American Values, 2005) p. 6.

major type of crime".[93] A similar study in the United States tracked every child born on the Hawaiian island of Kauai in 1955. Thirty years later, it identified that five out of every six of those children with an adult criminal record came from families where a parent was absent.[94]

However it is not just in the home where the lack of male role models has been linked to an increase in youth crime. The decline in male school teachers has been partially linked to increased incidences of robberies, assaults and weapons offences. Adolescent psychologist Michael Carr-Gregg stated:

> We know males give something different to the developing boy than what female teachers give. To some extent we have lost that male narrative and left it to Hollywood to teach boys about masculinity.[95]

If declining male teacher numbers can be linked to a rise in anti-social behaviour, one can scarcely overstate the catastrophic social cost of children being raised without fathers.

Support for the importance of the traditional family unit in the welfare of children was a key finding in research undertaken by Wendy Manning and Kathleen Lamb, and published in the *Journal of Marriage and Family*. Their research paper 'Adolescent Well-Being in Cohabiting, Married and Single-Parent Families', found that adolescents in married, two biological-parent families on the whole fared better than other

---

93 Bill Muehlenberg, 'Fatherlessness and Violence' (2011) <www.billmuehlenberg.com> (accessed 18 July 2013)

94 Emmy E. Werner, 'Risk, resilience, and recovery: Perspectives from the Kauai Longitudinal Study', *Development and Psychopathology* (1993) vol. 5, no. 4, p. 507 [doi:10.1017/S095457940000612X].

95 Michael Carr-Gregg cited in Peter Mickelburough, 'Boys missing a life lesson from male teachers' *Herald Sun* (online) (15 February 2010 at 12:00am) <www.heraldsun.com.au> (accessed 7 July 2013). Print edition not available to the writer.

children living in any of the alternative family types, including single mother, cohabiting stepfather, and married stepfather categories. Obviously, the advantage of marriage appears to exist primarily when the child is the biological offspring of both parents.[96]

Yet again we see social science confirming the so-called 'prejudices' of traditionalist social policy, but even though these finding have been on the books for at least a decade, 'progressives' seem oblivious to them. It seems that the 'progressives' are only interested in the science that validates leftist ideas. They are, therefore, the last group of political agitators in a position to lecture others about bias or prejudice, or claim that conservatives have nothing of use to contribute to the debate.

Mr Justice Coleridge of the UK Family Court noted that family breakdown is the cause of most social ills and that, despite its faults, marriage should be restored as the 'gold standard' and social stigma should be re-applied to those who destroy family life. He went on to say:

> What is a matter of private concern when it is on a small scale becomes a matter of public concern when it reaches epidemic proportions.[97]

Trapped as today's 'progressives' are in the discredited opinions of '60s radicalism, we cannot wait for them to take that leap into the future and deal with the root cause of these problems. This is because they have proven themselves incapable of recognising the brutal consequence of their policies upon society and the individual today. This is yet another reason why *we need a conservative revolution.*

---

96 Wendy Manning and Kathleen Lamb, 'Adolescent Well-Being in Cohabiting, Married, and Single Parent Families' *J Marriage Fam* (November, 2003) vol. 65 no. 4 pp. 876-893 [doi: 10.1111/j.1741-3737.2003.00876.x].

97 'Judge warns of epidemic of family breakdown' *The Telegraph* (online) (17 June 2013) <www.telegraph.co.uk> (accessed 7 July 2013) Print edition not available to the writer.

## Challenges to the traditional family in today's society and their consequences

Despite the evidence of the importance of marriage, biological attachment to children and the complementary nature of gender specific roles, the traditional family is under sustained attack from the radicals' agenda.

In February 2010, the Queensland Parliament introduced surrogacy laws allowing singles and same-sex couples to get a child 'of their own' using reproductive technology or surrogacy. In criticising the laws, Dr David van Gend highlighted that they allowed the child's birth certificate to be legally falsified to declare the single adult, or the same-sex couple to be the baby's true 'parents', even if it is patently obvious that there is no biological attachment.[98] Moreover, according to Australian ethicist Professor Margaret Somerville:

> It is one matter for children not to know their genetic identity as a result of unintended circumstances. It is quite another matter to deliberately destroy children's links to their biological parents, and especially for society to be complicit in this destruction.[99]

The left's social engineering raises a number of questions. Should the state be *deliberately* legislating to deprive children of having both a mother and father? What message does that send to future generations about the importance of these vital roles? Are the rights of the child the primary concern of those who advocate for a move away from the traditional family?

---

98 David van Gend, 'Next stolen generation – who needs a mother anyway?' *Newsweekly* (online) (6 March 2010) <newsweekly.com.au> (accessed 7 July 2013). Print edition not available to the writer.
99 Margaret Somerville cited in David van Gend, *ibid.*

These concerns are put into perspective by writer Ryan T. Anderson:

> Redefining marriage would further distance marriage from the needs of children and deny the importance of mothers and fathers. It would deny, as a matter of policy, the ideal that children need a mother and father … it would be very difficult for the law to send a message that *fathers matter when it has redefined marriage to make fathers optional.*[100]

The left's blind ambition to fundamentally diminish the importance of the traditional family can have adverse consequences for children. Children in families without a married mother and father can miss out on the benefits (as discussed earlier) of having married biological parents in their lives. They are more likely to suffer poorer health outcomes, such as higher rates of mental health disorders, mortality rates and long-standing illnesses, and are more likely to be exposed to abuse and neglect.[101] A Deakin University study found that children with a step-parent were 17 times more likely to die from violence.[102] Australian forensic psychologist Lillian De Bortoli concludes that children face an increased risk of physical abuse if they live with one biological parent and one non-biological parent.[103]

---

100 Ryan T. Anderson, 'Marriage Matters: Consequences of Redefining Marriage', Issue Brief for The Heritage Foundation (online) (18 March 2013) <www.heritage.org> (accessed 31 July 2013).

101 Steve Smallwood and Ben Wilson (ed.), 'Focus on Families', *British Office of National Statistics* (Palgrave Macmillan, 2007) pp. 58, 65 and David de Vaus, 'Diversity and change in Australian families: statistical profiles', Australian Institute of Family Studies (2004) pp. 63-64.

102 Andrew Trounson, 'Children "safer with biological parent"', *The Australian* (online) (7 May 2008) <www.theaustralian.com.au> (accessed 31 July 2013). Print edition not available to writer.

103 Candace Sutton, 'Australian study into children more likely to die a violent death', *News.com.au* (online) (6 May 2013) <www.news.com.au> (accessed 31 July 2013). Print edition not available to writer.

Such findings are not meant to pass judgment on or criticise the many different Australian families that do their best in raising children; the findings aim to identify the risk factors in order to help improve the lives of children. They also demonstrate the extreme folly of the left in dismissing the importance of the traditional family. The left have the evidence of the risks to children before them and yet they continue to pursue their radical agenda and dismiss any critical examination of what they are proposing.

The Australian Broadcasting Corporation (ABC) – an organisation funded by Australian taxpayers – seems to be a cheerleader for environments that are potentially less than optimal for children. In a recent example, the ABC's desperation to justify the left's 'anything goes' family agenda resulted in shock and embarrassment after they had initially celebrated two men who paid a surrogate in Russia to have a child which they then took back to Australia.[104] A few years later, these two men were arrested for sexually abusing the child and permitting sexual abuse of the child by others.

Queensland Detective Inspector Jon Rouse stated: "What's pretty sad about this one is the way this child came into their lives. It's just really a tragedy. It's extremely depraved."[105]

D.I. Rouse is right, this whole episode is depraved, but I would

104 Ginger Gorman, 'Two Dads Are Better Than One' *Australian Broadcasting Corporation – Far North Queensland* via Google Cache (23 June 2013 at 11:34:45) <webcache.googleusercontent.com> (accessed 9 July 2013). This piece has been pulled from the *ABC's* website. Nevertheless, conservative activists online have captured and saved the content as well as related media for the public's benefit. See for example: Anonymous, '"Two Dads Are Better Than One": Pro-Gay Adoption ABC Profile of Convicted Pedophile' *Wintery Knight* (blog) (1 July 2013 at 6:00pm) <winteryknight.wordpress.com> (accessed 9 July 2013).
105 'Adopted Boy Sexually Abused by Gay Fathers', *Sky News* (online) (3 July 2013 at 12:51pm) <news.sky.com> (accessed 9 July 2013).

say that the way the child came 'into the lives' of these two men is the 'progressive' cheering of such ideas by the politically correct and therefore ignorant mainstream press.

This is not to deny that abuse also occurs in normative families. But this does not mean that we should potentially expose more children to negative consequences by expanding the risks that they may be exposed to with reckless policy and irresponsible politics. In general, normative families have proven themselves indispensable to society; they must be reinforced, empowered and supported.

Social policy should continue to advocate for the best possible social environment for children. More often than not, as studies have shown, that environment is a family with the child's married biological mother and father. Of course, there will always be exceptions to this – some traditional families fail miserably at child care and some step families do a wonderful job of raising children – but it should not deter society as a whole from encouraging its citizens to pursue the traditional family model.

Competent social policy should be drafted by those who understand the primacy of natural law and who are able to see patterns in society. Those who do not have this ability should have no role in social reform. Unfortunately, the politically correct environment we inhabit makes this competence almost impossible because noticing some patterns may result in slanderous accusations of bigotry and intolerance. This is a recipe for bad social policy and disastrous legal reform.

Further damage to the family unit is commissioned in other ways by leftist ideologues. For example, the rise of government programs designed to supplant the traditional familial responsibilities has also undermined the family structure. If government is prepared to reduce the instance of hardship associated with family breakdown, then less importance is placed on maintaining a relationship by those involved in it. Even well-meaning programs that have the welfare of the child at their heart can serve to reduce the importance of family in our society.

One example is the growing 'school breakfast program.' Under this program, hundreds of schools now provide breakfast for their students. The Australian Red Cross alone provides breakfast for students in 263 schools.[106] While the intention is a well-meaning, benevolent one, and seeks to redress a perceived injustice, replacing the parent's responsibility to feed their own children with the state is a small but significant step in devolving the importance of family life. Having a state bureaucracy assume parental responsibility does nothing to reinforce or encourage such a responsibility among parents; in fact, it only damages it further.

So too has the state undermined the importance of maintaining strong families in the reduction of funding support for Family Relationship Centres. These centres do no harm to the maintenance of parental and spousal responsibility. Despite the success of these centres in dealing with the problems that affect family relationships, tens of millions of dollars in support was withdrawn by the federal Labor government. This is despite the overwhelming evidence that strong marriages and stable families are good for society and a benefit to taxpayers.

The financial cost of marriage breakdown can be assessed by the billions of dollars spent on federal, state and local government

---

106 Carol Nader and Farrah Tomazin, 'Waiting list grows for school breakfast clubs', *The Age* (21 October 2008) p. 3.

programs dealing with the consequences of broken homes.[107] This alone should be enough for politicians of all persuasions to support marriage and the traditional family as being important to our society.

Regrettably, the social cost is even more staggering yet it goes almost unremarked by many of our political leaders. For too many of them, to attribute a link between our failing families and escalating social disorder would be to pass judgment on the radical social experiments of the past fifty years and find them wanting.

I believe that instead of cowering before a morally and economically bankrupt ideology, we must strive for the ideal by implementing the timeless principles which have successfully served our communities in the past.

While it is clear that the unrelenting attack on traditional marriage and the natural family has had a significant negative impact on our societal standards, many of the public statements of the social radicals have gone virtually unchallenged. Conservatives cannot allow that to continue. The importance of marriage and the traditional family needs to be publically recognised as the absolute bedrock of our communities and the ideal toward which we must strive. The benefits of doing so and the consequences of failure are evidenced by the failing social compact that is a product of the radical social agenda.

---

107 An Australian House of Representatives Committee report of 1998 concluded that "[m]arriage and family breakdown costs the Australian nation at least $3 billion each year." House of Representatives Standing Committee on Legal and Constitutional Affairs, *To have and to hold: Strategies to strengthen marriage and relationships* (1998) p. 52. The Australian Department of Families, Housing, Community Services and Indigenous Affairs has since concluded that "it is likely that this amount has increased." FaHCSIA Social Policy Research Paper Series, 'Number 35: Marriage breakdown in Australia: social correlates, gender and initiator status' (as updated at 4 June 2013) <www.fahcsia.gov.au> (accessed 19 July 2013).

The current cost and the future risk to our national wellbeing are too great. We simply cannot afford to remain silent about the importance of the traditional family in shaping a positive future for our nation. To restore public belief in the vital role of marriage and the traditional family to our society will require conservatives to publicly engage in their defence. It will require politicians and political parties to cease the appeasement of a vocal and bitter minority who actively seek to compromise these cornerstones of our society. It will require leaders prepared to reaffirm that discriminating in favour of traditional marriage and the natural family is in our national interest. This is why *we need a conservative revolution.*

# 4

# The Third Pillar: Our Flag

Today's world is a restless one, defined as much by its turmoil as the constant striving for stability among its people. Australia remains an example to other nations for its wholehearted historical embrace of the democratic principle, mainstream values and a culture that has emphasised personal liberty as well as individual responsibility, both of which foster a unique communitarian spirit among our fellow citizens. Our spirit – one of persistence, resilience and mateship – has unified us in battle and continues to underpin our international relationships.

All of these ideas are reflected in our national symbols. One of these is the most pervasive and the most powerful – the Australian flag. Our flag flies proudly throughout our community: above schools, businesses, iconic buildings and sporting fields. We usually give it no more than a passing glance. But it is important to consider closely what our flag represents and to make every effort to protect it.

Our flag is part of our collective identity. Within its weave, its colours and its design is the entire history of our nation and the people who have called it their 'home.' Changing symbols that go to the root or core of the national identity are not reform; changes such as these are an act of vandalism, a radical assault on the foundations on which our country has grown to be the envy of our regional neighbours. Abolishing the flag is essentially a repudiation of the principles on which our greatness rests. Replacing our flag with another would involve much more than just updating a design or airbrushing out our British heritage; it would inflict the woes of an amnesiac upon us all – like forgetting one's parents. Only the radical is wilfully and maliciously forsaking his patrimony; this is a moral crime, and one which a people will ultimately pay for by a loss of community consciousness, and therefore a loss of direction.

Naturally, because conservatives have an interest in supporting those things that reinforce a strong and confident community, we also recognise the activities that threaten to compromise our moral strength such as attempts to undermine our national symbols.

The security and prospects Australians enjoy today have not arrived by accident. Indeed, a strong Australia, built upon the bedrock of a strong national identity was uppermost in the minds of our founding fathers.

Sir Henry Parkes, widely considered as the 'father of federation' captured this sentiment clearly when he spoke at the Constitutional Conference in 1890:

> There is not one of these important colonies which has not felt the wonderful stimulus given to industry, to every kind of enterprise, to education, to refinement in social manners, and in the estimates of moral life which have been going on, until we are now in a condition that we may be contrasted favourably with some of the wealthiest states in the world, not only in respect of our enterprise, our skill, and our industrial vigour, but also in the higher walks of life … if we acknowledge that bond which unites us as one people … if we acknowledge that kinship from which we cannot escape and from which no one desires to escape – if we acknowledge that, and if we subordinate all lower and sectional considerations to the one great aim of building

up a power which, in the world outside, will have more influence, command more respect, enhance every comfort, and every profit of life amongst ourselves – if we only enter into the single contemplation of this one object, the thing will be accomplished, and accomplished more easily, and in a shorter time, than any great achievement of the same nature that was ever accomplished before.[108]

Parkes knew what a united Australia could achieve by focusing on the interests of the Australian people. Through the strength of their resolve, the nation's influence in affairs external to our domestic concerns would grow. At the same conference, Alfred Deakin also spoke of the potential of fostering Australian patriotism:

This sentiment of our nationality is one which, I believe, we shall see increasing in its intensity year by year, and it will count for much more than it does now when the people of these colonies have become a people sprung from the coil, a people the vast majority of whom will know no other home than the soil of Australia. I believe that this passion of nationality will widen and deepen and strengthen its tides until they will far more than suffice to float all the burdens that may be placed upon their bosom.[109]

We need to continue to build upon the sentiments that forged a nation (and our nationality) by defending that which is uniquely ours. Paramount is the need to protect those institutions and traditions that have served our country so well, from those who would seek to dismantle them.

Defending Australia's sovereignty, our Constitution, the rule of

---

108 *Official Record of the Proceedings and Debates of the Australasian Federation Conference, Melbourne 1890* (University of Sydney Library, 1999) pp. 37 ff.
109 *Ibid.*, p. 72.

law, our social order and traditional values, fostering patriotism and supporting our federalist system of government, all these form the theoretical cornerstones of the conservative revolution. It should come as no surprise that they are also the cornerstones of our nation.

These institutions and principles have shaped our nation since federation and guided us through many challenging times. They have proved their enduring value in a world of rapid change. Of course, the difficulties of times past are not always directly relevant to what society faces today, but these vital pillars of our society remain no less relevant because they are rooted in the timeless ideas that transcend temporary fashions and momentary public whims. Through them, we have a unified national spirit (what is sometimes colloquially referred to as 'Our Story'), with which we can rise to meet the identifiable challenges of today as well as those of tomorrow.

Meeting these challenges means standing up for Australia's interests and being resolute and focused on that task. Bowing to the external threats from other nations or those of a vocal minority that abuses the tolerance and liberty that are part of our cultural heritage only serves to encourage further and further demands which, as we have seen over the last several decades, become less and less reasonable over time. Indeed, while the conservative acknowledges that events may trigger responses he recognises that they must not be the only thing to do so.

I have argued in this short volume that the task ahead is to build on the conservative foundations of our forefathers. This means acknowledging and accepting that our role in world affairs, whether it be in foreign aid, international security or responding appropriately to the calls of our allies and friends abroad, depends entirely on our moral stability and material prosperity at home. It also means that we should never compromise Australia's national interest upon the altar of international pressure.

For too long, we have been governed by a political class that has confused and neglected these important issues. This is why *we need a conservative revolution*.

## Australia's sovereignty

Defending Australia's sovereignty is a critical responsibility for the conservative political class. In recent times there has been more and more pressure brought to bear from lobby groups, international organisations and dysfunctional governments for Australia to cede some decision-making powers to external organisations.

Most recently, the international pressure to be part of an ineffective response to global warming would have seen billions of Australian taxpayers' dollars go to unaccountable bodies such as the United Nations or other subsidiary transnational organisations for redistribution to any number of corrupt or failed nation states. The fact that the former Australian Government was prepared to accede to such demands, despite the huge disadvantage to our own citizens, for fear of allegedly damaging its international reputation, strongly suggests that our national interest is not always served by those who govern the Treasury benches. Clearly, as the political risks increase the conservative voter must become more wary of whom he supports at the polling booth.

Government should not be afraid of making decisions that promote our nation's interests, even if they do not meet with universal acclaim. Burke was right speaking to the electors of Bristol in 1774, and he would be right speaking that same truth to us today. Trying to please everyone will only serve to ultimately compromise our status and respect within the international community.

Likewise, while our nation should always strive to maintain good standing within the global community, it should not do so at the risk of our sovereignty being subsumed by third party demands or unaccountable bureaucracies that seek to drive international consensus to further their own agenda. Nations achieve respect through co-operation, but also by standing alone when necessary, to protect their national interest.

Those who so easily concede to foreign demands and surrender their rights of self-governance and self-determination (no matter how trivial that surrender or those rights may seem at the time) are hardly worthy of respect, and rarely if ever receive it. If the 20th century has taught us anything, it is that international relations are governed by the law of the jungle; in the law of the jungle, prestige is gained only by those with the courage and will to have a voice of their own and act accordingly. I would rather that Australia earn its prestige by standing sovereign and strong, rather than following the misguided fashionable trends of the day.

Conservative author Dinesh D'Souza, in his book *Letters to a Young Conservative*, described the benefit of national self-interest when he wrote:

> The people in democratic society empower their government to act in their interest. Why should their elected representatives be neutral between their interests and, say, the interests of the Somalians? To ask a nation to ignore its own self-interest is tantamount to asking it to put aside the welfare of its people.[110]

As Parkes and Deakin identified over a century ago, the future strength of Australia relies on its people to support our nation and the national self-interest. The unifying spirit that comes from national pride, shared values and a sense of civic responsibility are vital to our continuing strength.

---

110 Dinesh D'Souza, *Letter to a Young Conservative* (Basic Books, 2002) p. 207.

It is often said that Australia is the 'lucky country.' A country free of civil unrest, where we can live in peace and with the freedom to live the way we choose. But as citizens and residents of this great country we also have responsibilities.

We have responsibilities to be law-abiding people, to do our part to improve on those things that make Australia a prosperous, wealthy, and competitive country. This is true of those who were born here as well as for those who have chosen to make Australia home.

Many migrants come to Australia for a better life, what one may describe as the 'Australian way of life.' It is, of course, understandable that many migrants seek to maintain some of their own culture and customs in their new life here, but it is also important that they adopt the culture and practices that make us uniquely Australian. Our society is strengthened when our newest citizens learn about how our traditions, our shared values, culture and language have shaped our nation. This process should not be shunned or denounced, as it is by the radical; it should be embraced and celebrated as a source of strength, which it certainly can be.

Respecting the importance of the worldview and the practices which inform the culture of our society helps ensure that the liberties we enjoy are properly contextualised in order to limit their misuse or abuse. In the words of former Prime Minister John Howard:

> our celebration of diversity must not be at the expense of the common values that bind us together as one people ... Nor should it be at the expense of the ongoing pride in what are commonly regarded as the values, traditions and accomplishments of the old Australia. A sense of shared values is our social cement. Without it we risk a society

governed by coercion rather than consent. That is not an
Australia any of us would want to live in.[111]

A failure to defend Australian culture, or to respect the institutions
that have stood the test of time, could result in the creation of a very
different country, one that is not only unfamiliar but hostile to the
things we hold dear. Instead of a unified and cohesive community
– built on common values, goals, a sense of belonging and working
together – a disparate Australia could emerge, comprised of isolated
groups competing against each other, seeking to further their own
aims at the expense of others.

In fact, there is evidence that this is already emerging in parts of
Australian society today. To prevent its metastasis, we need to reaffirm
the role of our enduring institutions and ensure the values on which
a stable and prosperous nation depends are encouraged with a view
to their being universally and voluntarily upheld by society as a whole.

This is why *we need a conservative revolution*.

## The Australian Constitution

A large part of Australia's national strength and stability can be
directly linked to our founding document – the Constitution. This
primary document affirmed our status as a nation built upon the rock
of a uniquely British variant of European Christian civilisation, in
particular, one that is established 'under God'. The practical effect
is that our constitutional order is not just subject to the whim of the
people but has as its central organising principle a liberty that revolves
around an idea which transcends individual desire or personal whim.
We derive our concept of justice which is impersonal and objective

---

111 John Howard, Australia Day address to the National Press Club, 'A Profound Truth
and a Simple Irony', Commonwealth Parliament House, Canberra ACT (25 January
2006).

from this relationship between the citizen and the law. To help guarantee this liberty and avoid tyranny, executive power was apportioned under the Constitution across various levels of government and under the stability of the Crown. What many people seem to forget today, even many conservatives themselves, is that the value of the Crown resides in the fact that it is a non-political institution which, but for the defamatory campaign to unjustly discredit it, can embody the spirit of the nation and therefore arguably represent the people on a more profound level than a Member of Parliament.

It is significant that the federation of the six Australian colonies to form the Commonwealth of Australia in 1901 was a result of a direct vote of the people, the first time in history a nation had been formed in this manner. In short, our Constitution was drawn up by Australians, for Australians and was endorsed by Australians through a series of referenda.[112]

This Australian Constitution adopted aspects of the four existing federations – the United States, Switzerland, Canada and Germany – to create what many would consider to be the finest constitution in the world: our nation has been blessed by being spared the civil turmoils of other countries in the now democratic world; our only major constitutional crisis in 1975 was resolved through established parliamentary and electoral processes without the bloodshed and chaos that may have accompanied similar troubles in other neighbouring states.

In combining aspects of other federalist systems of government, the founding fathers were able to build on the wisdom of our ancestors. It is a point of pride that the very genesis of our nation was the product of quintessentially conservative minds who looked

112 The Hon Rod Kemp, *Australia's Future: Constitutional Monarchy or Constitutional Chaos?* (Liberal Party of Australia, 1991) p. 1.

to established traditions and drew from what worked among other peoples whose countries shared a similar cultural and religious foundation.

By adopting that which had proved itself to be of enduring significance in the affairs of nationhood, including the separation of powers, an executive that remains as part of the legislature, population-based electorates, equal state representation in the Senate and a formal process through which the Constitution could be changed, their conservative approach has been vindicated over many decades.

Constitutions are meant to be enduring documents and ours has brought us through two World Wars, a depression, a major constitutional crisis and various political controversies with flying colours. It has delivered over a century of political stability in a world where corruption, political turmoil and civil war are all too apparent.

Critics of the Constitution should be reminded that after having been promulgated in 1901, it has provided us with stability during what could be described as the most turbulent and bloody century of the Western historical narrative. This is no small achievement, yet the radical reformer will have us believe that we must shed the wisdom of the founding fathers, ignore their lessons, and throw away the fruit of their work. In return we are to embrace the utopian abstracts of revolutionary thinkers who draw their inspiration from the French Revolution and its enduring symbol: the guillotine.

The fact that our Constitution has been relatively unchanged for over one hundred years, with only 13 separate amendments, while our country has grown and prospered so spectacularly is testament to the relevance of the founding fathers and their lessons today.[113]

---

113 *YES/No Referendum '99*, Official Referendum pamphlet (Australian Electoral Commission, 1999) p. 17.

The conservative recognises the importance of the Constitution in providing safeguards and protection to our freedoms and security. Changes to this most vital of documents should not be haphazard and those who argue for any proposed amendments to it bear a very high onus of proof as to why those changes are truly necessary. It is not for the conservative to argue against change here, it is for the radical to convince us that those changes will be beneficial and will not damage the liberties that we have been guaranteed to date. Simply put, if no such assurances are given, no change can be accepted.

There is one aspect of our Constitution that should be considered absolutely vital in protecting and conserving our system of government. That is our constitutional monarchy.

## Constitutional monarchy

In Australia, the Crown is the symbol of the state and is represented in Australia by the Governor-General – an office established under the Constitution.

The Constitution confers three categories of power on the office of the Governor-General. There are those relating to their responsibilities for administering the government, those powers that may be assigned to them by the Sovereign and the reserve powers of the Crown.

It is important to recognise that there was (and remains) no reference to the Sovereign as head of state in the Australian Constitution. Indeed it appears our founding fathers deliberately chose to eschew the term and, through section 61 of the Constitution, assign the Governor-General powers that had hitherto not been given to any Governor or Governor-General anywhere else in the Commonwealth.

Section 61 details that executive power is vested in the Crown but is exercisable by the Governor-General, in essence providing the

Governor-General with all the powers of head of state.

The duty of the Sovereign in Australia's Constitution is to appoint the Governor-General on the advice of the Prime Minister. While the Sovereign can also remove the commission of the Governor-General on the Prime Minister's advice, they are able to seek further advice in relation to this decision. This allows any such decision to be delayed and provide an opportunity for action to be taken against a government leader who is abusing his office.

Thus the Crown provides a constitutional safeguard that is above the day to day machinations of politics. The Crown provides a stable foundation for the sustained construction of nationhood.

As the sixth oldest democracy in the world, Australia is testament to the success of the constitutional monarchy as a stable and continuing form of government. Only the United Kingdom, United States, Canada, New Zealand and Switzerland have a longer democratic tradition than Australia – most of which are also constitutional monarchies. It is telling that these other democracies share a common cultural and religious patrimony; clearly, there is something in these traditions that is not only conducive to the maintenance of a stable democratic order, but essential to its creation. This validates the conservative suspicion, as discussed earlier in this volume, of any move to abolish our traditions or claims that they are 'anachronistic' or 'irrelevant' for the citizens of a modern Australia.

Those who seek to radically change the nature of the Australian Constitution by removing the role of the Crown and establishing an Australian republic have repeatedly failed to successfully prosecute their case before the Australian people, with the resultant dwindling support for their cause. This was most recently demonstrated by the 1999 republic referendum, where, after extensive consultation, the republican movement put forward a model that was overwhelmingly rejected by the Australian people. Some have argued that the reason why the referendum failed was because the republican movement itself was split along the line of which model to assume as their proposed alternative to the status quo. Whatever the reason may be, since their failure they have confined their advocacy to 'a republic at any cost'[114], any sort of republic, as long as we get one. This does not illustrate a movement that believes in the good of its proposed reform; rather it demonstrates that they are motivated by simple hatred: 'anything but this' they shout, despite the fact that their freedom to advocate constitutional vandalism has been established and guaranteed by the very thing they seek to wreck.

The conservative is forced to reject this type of irrationality as imprudent, illogical and dangerous. There are many types of republics in the world including the United States, Switzerland, Ireland, Zimbabwe and France (which has had five!). To claim that *any* republic will do is to wilfully ignore some of the most important aspects of national governance and stability. Indeed, while the pro-republican cause seems to rest upon emotive opposition to our existing constitutional arrangements, they are seeking to put the monarchy on trial rather than test the merit of their own arguments.

The simple fact that our existing constitutional arrangements have already been proven to successfully rise above all challenges appears to have been lost on the intellectual elites within the republican movement.

The Crown is central to the stability of our Constitution. To replace it, in whatever form, may put at risk the very system that is the envy of the democratic world. Some will maintain that what the

---

114 Senate Finance and Public Administration Committee, Parliament of Australia, Plebiscite for an Australian Republic Bill 2008 (29 April 2009) p. 15.

republicans have proposed previously are minimalist amendments to the Constitution and that not much would actually change. This fiction ignores the reality that the 1999 republican model would have required 69 separate changes to our nation's foundational document – and that's the so-called 'minimalist' republican model. To put that into perspective, as noted there have only ever been 13 separate amendments to our Constitution since federation, which should tell us that the minimalist agenda of the republicans is in fact a radical overhaul of the existing system.[115]

That said, conservatives are not uniformly against change. We recognise that flexibility in the application of the principles we hold to be timeless is vital to the continuation of society as circumstances change and shifting challenges may demand an appropriate shift in policy. However, as has been argued earlier, the desire for change must be balanced against the interests of our society. In other words, the alternative must be better than that already available.

But change also entails risks – some that are immediately identifiable and others that cannot be reasonably foreseen. In the light of those risks, and even if we accept the republicans' assurances that not much will change, one simple question remains: if the alternative is only as good as the current system, what is the point in changing? The answer to this rhetorical question may shed further light on the true intentions and motivation of the radical 'reformer'.

The official answers provided by the republican cause are mostly comprised of pithy phrases and marshmallow symbolism that more resembles a populist advertising campaign than the sober contemplation of a national constitution. That, too, is telling.

---

115 For an exploration of the history and issues surrounding the push for an Australian Republic, see: David Smith, *Head of State – the Governor General, the Monarchy, the Republic and the Dismissal* (MacLeay, 2005).

Whatever an Australian republic may do, there are very many things it won't do and can't do. An Australian republic won't create jobs. It won't improve trade. It won't improve the economy or our international relations. It won't enhance our prestige as a nation and it won't make us any more sovereign than we already are and have been since the passage of the *Australia Acts* in 1986. It won't improve the way we live, but it may actually jeopardise the very stability that has become a hallmark of our democracy.

In a world of political instability, where Australia stands as a beacon of light to the democratic world, where we are fortunate to be governed by a system that protects us and allows us to live in peace and safety, the conservative asks 'why would anyone forsake a proven success for a radical experiment and not expect there to be significant consequences?' Such questions are not asked often enough, and the answers that are given are woeful. This is why *we need a conservative revolution*.

## Decentralisation of power

In safeguarding individual liberty, one of the aims of our Constitution, and the role of the Crown under it, is to deny the concentration of power in any single individual, group or legislature. This is achieved through the separation of powers between the Parliament (which wields the legislative power), the Executive Government (the executive power) and the Judicature (judicial power). Additional protection is also offered by the nature of our federalist system through which specific powers are allocated between state and federal governments.

At the federal level, the parliament acts as a check on the executive, as no government can stand without the ongoing confidence of the House of Representatives. The Senate, with its equal representation from each of the six states, acts as a further legislative counterweight to the powers of the federal government.

The Constitution also granted specific responsibilities to the states, which, in turn, have their own parliamentary systems of accountability comprising (in most instances) two houses of parliament. In many instances, a further devolution of powers has evolved through state governments to local government, with many of these directly assuming responsibilities for the needs and requirements of their communities.

The division of power and responsibility across these three levels of government has caused some to claim that our nation is over-governed.

There is no doubt that great administrative savings could be made through the removal of layers of bureaucracy and preventing the duplication of administration. To the conservative, this has an enduring appeal as it reduces the overall size of government, making it more efficient and less intrusive. The challenge, however, is how to achieve this without compromising the protections and restraint against unfettered power that our federalist system provides.

In some areas, a consistent and uniform approach to regulation may be justified. However, such accommodations shouldn't extend to areas where states can compete with each other on service provision or taxation. Where states can reduce their taxation burden, thereby making themselves more attractive to potential new residents and businesses, they should be encouraged to do so. States should also have the continuing freedom to determine their own policies in other areas such as education and health because these are areas which benefit from decentralisation. This is because different systems are tried, tested, and the successful ones are mimicked or improved in a competitive environment. This adds to the vibrancy, diversity and flexibility of the national system and strengthens the country.

If competition or the mismanagement of taxpayer funds results in a decrease in service provision, the conservative would argue that the Commonwealth should resist the temptation to intervene, lest the accountability of the state government to their respective constituents be lessened.

The decentralisation of power only works effectively when there is a clear separation of roles and responsibilities, honouring and giving rise to accountability in and by the electorate. Where there is insufficient distinction of the responsibilities of each of the various levels of government, it is difficult to hold to account those responsible for their actions.

The temptation for citizens and polity alike is always to blame those further up the chain with the expectation that the next tier of government will fix whatever problem is vexing society. In recent decades this has been the case in Australia with the subsequent result being that the public cannot readily identify (nor do they care to) which level of government is failing them.

In the demand for a quick political fix to a systemic problem, responsibility moves toward the larger body. The inevitable consequence of such disregard for the separation of powers is that real power, effective power, will ultimately rest with far too few.

There is no doubt that the years since federation have seen major change in the operational responsibilities of government. The conservative has and should always strive to pursue a path that prevents both tyranny, through the concentration of power, and anarchy, where individual freedom reigns untempered.

In seeking to balance the desire for individual freedom and order simultaneously with the need for government efficiency and effectiveness, the clear separation of powers as enshrined in our Constitution helps to ensure that the potential loss of freedom is always kept at least a generation away. This important principle of good governance seems to have been forgotten in the rush for power and influence. This is why *we need a conservative revolution.*

# 5

# The Fourth Pillar: Free Enterprise

Free enterprise is the driving force for personal and national prosperity. A system based on this principle offers the only economic model whereby individuals and businesses can own outright or have an interest in the resources required to produce goods and services, actually produce those goods and services for profit and make available their personal labour for payment.

Under such a system no external coercion is needed to force creativity, productivity or innovation. Rather it is the pursuit of individual satisfaction and profit that drives these things. Accordingly, free enterprise and an order which respects private property rights as fundamental to individual and national prosperity and security, are the systems most compatible with individual freedom and political democracy.

Conservatives support free enterprise and capitalism primarily because these ideas have generated more wealth and lifted more people out of poverty than any other political or economic ideology. I say 'primarily' because any problems encountered in the modern political order which are often blamed on capitalism or free market ideas are, on closer inspection, often caused by abuses of state or corporate power, institutional disrespect of the concepts of human dignity, or failures and anomalies in regulatory regimes. I believe the earlier sections of this volume have demonstrated the need for the promotion and maintenance of a healthy moral culture. Indeed, capitalism and the free market functions best in a society which has a strong moral backbone. Failures here can more often than not be traced to the failures of the morality without which no society can function, no matter which economic, political or social order its traditions demand.

The conservative position today is that our traditions require us to pursue an economic system based on the primacy of the individual while also respecting his role in society. A balance needs to be set. Indeed, capitalism and support for free enterprise are an entwined political system because they replace the collectivist ideals attached to socialism with the reward for individual productivity and innovation.

History has demonstrated that lower tax and a greater emphasis on personal responsibility and individual autonomy is in the best interests of a free and prosperous nation. Such attitudes also restrict the growth of government and the progressive intrusion of the state into the wellbeing of the individual. Rather than increasing the size of government and its regulatory powers, as is the preferred method of the political left, the conservative understands that greater support for individual choice and providing reward for personal achievement are the keys to a stronger economy because it shifts the incentive from fear of state coercion and punishment to self-motivation for reward.

Increasing incentives for work and productivity provides benefits to both individual citizens and the greater community. Oddly, the non-conservative often finds such notions objectionable. In a short piece published at *Forbes* magazine, Dinesh D'Souza asked:

> Why should people feel aggrieved that the rich are pulling further ahead if they are also moving forward? If you drive

a Mercedes and I have to walk, that's a radical difference in lifestyle. But is it a big deal if you drive a Mercedes and I drive a Hyundai? If I have a four bedroom condo, should I be morally outraged that you have a 12 bedroom house?[116]

Despite the logic of such a position, the radicals, 'progressives' and other leftists are often consumed by the politics of envy and conclude that one can only achieve great wealth or independent financial security by taking advantage of others. This morbid attitude relegates success (especially the individual's enjoyment of his success) to the status of a fraud perpetrated on others; it suggests that no person can get ahead unless his advancement is somehow made at the expense of his hapless neighbour. It does not take much to see that no society run along these lines is capable of achieving the self-motivated prosperity necessary for wealth acquisition, as well as the scientific, technological and economic development and innovation needed for *genuine progress*.

Of course all systems are liable to abuse. But the abuse of or departure from the principles of a healthy, stable and centred society described in this volume should not be taken as evidence of the moral bankruptcy of those principles themselves. It is either narrow-minded or thoughtless to suggest that because problems or anomalies may be experienced in a free market or capitalist system, that the whole system and its theoretical foundations should be shed and replaced with the ideology of socialism, even if in some watered down version.

The theories the radical or 'progressive' would like to have dominate the political and economic discourse in the West have been the cause of misery for countless millions in the 20th century, and across the whole globe; in some remote parts of the developing world,

---

116 Dinesh D'Souza, 'The Moral Limits of Wealth'. *Forbes* (online) <www.forbes.com> (9 October 2000, accessed 19 June 2013). Print edition not available to the writer.

they continue to wreak their destructive force on its people, keeping them enslaved and poor. As this volume goes to press, the centralist, bureaucratic and big-government economies of Europe continue to throw that transnational experiment further into question. With so many concrete examples of failure, why is the radical so obsessed in repeating the inevitable disaster here?

Viewed from the perspective of individualism and communitarianism together, capitalism, while seen by some as a haven for greed, has as its core motivation the satisfaction of others' desires and needs. For it is through this process that the independent capitalist can achieve his own personal goals. Effectively, capitalism and the spirit of entrepreneurship channels human greed into the satisfaction of the desires of others through a system of free and voluntary exchange.

It is true to suggest that not all human desires can be considered moral or worthy of satisfaction. This is a judgment that the conservative is confident in making, for reasons explained earlier. However, the poor or misguided – yet free and voluntary – choices that an individual can make is a reflection on the human condition rather than an indictment of the free enterprise ethos. One could even conceive that the process whereby the 'true' is 'tried', as described by John Kekes in the opening section of this volume, is itself a kind of moral market place where tradition is refined over time and the collective wisdom of our forefathers reinforces, tempers and shapes our cultural heritage.

Perhaps one reason why critics of capitalism fall into error is because they tend to focus on the result – the personal wealth or success of the entrepreneur – rather than the principles behind the rationale, and the process involved. Because of this narrow-mindedness caused by the politics of envy, the 'progressive' ends up promoting a system that actually makes slaves of the people by making them further dependent on the state for their economic survival.

Adam Smith is regarded by some as the pioneer of modern free market economics. In his perhaps best known work, *The Wealth of Nations* (1775-1776), he wrote the following illustrative passage:

> It is not from the benevolence of the butcher, the brewer, or the baker, that we expect our dinner, but from their own interest. We address ourselves, not to their humanity, but to their self-love, and never talk to them of our own necessities, but of their advantages. Nobody but a beggar chooses to depend chiefly on the benevolence of his fellow citizens. Even a beggar does not depend on it entirely. The charity of well-disposed people, indeed, supplies him with the whole fund of his subsistence. But though this principle ultimately provides him with all the necessities of life which he has occasion for, it neither does nor can provide him with them as he has occasion for them.[117]

This shows how the self-interested instincts of the individual are channelled and focused in such a way as to benefit society as a whole. Far from liberating the poor or empowering the disenfranchised, the 'beggar' on the other hand becomes the perpetual slave in the 'progressive' order as he has no incentive other than to continue his dependence on the 'benevolence' of his neighbour. We have seen where this enforced benevolence leads: from the terrors of state socialism in 20th century Eastern Europe to the economic bankruptcy of many statist bureaucracies of 21st century Western Europe – it is truly frightening to think that well-intentioned leftists want to bring a version of this chaos to Australia, today.

---

117 Adam Smith, *The Wealth of Nations* bk. I ch. II (Hambling and Seyfang, 1811) vol. I, p. 19.

How do we avoid this chaos, and what is the conservative to do to ensure that we don't fall into the same trap of collectivist dependency? Put simply, the champions of such entrepreneurship are the small business owners.

## Small business

While there are many definitions of 'small business', in the public mind a small business is often one with twenty or fewer full time employees. Above this level, an enterprise is often large enough to have independent units dealing with financial accounts, human resources, personnel and sales. The small business, on the other hand, is often driven by an individual or close knit group of colleagues (sometimes a small or extended family) who are responsible for growing sales, strategic planning and business administration, often with little or no other internal support. For the purposes of this volume, this is broadly my understanding of the threshold of what a small business is.

Small business is the lifeblood of any democratic capitalist society. In Australia, small business is the major employer in our communities outside the monolithic government public sector. Recent estimates indicate there are in excess of two million small businesses operating in Australia who collectively employ almost *five million* Australians.[118] These entrepreneurial men and women identify under-serviced or over-priced markets and then invest their time, ingenuity and money in an attempt to offer alternative and competitive goods and services, and of course profit from their endeavours.

There are also individuals who effectively create an entirely new

---

118 *Australian Small Business – Key Statistics and Analysis* (Department of Industry, Innovation, Climate Change, Science, Research and Tertiary Education, Commonwealth of Australia, December 2012) p. 23.

market by rousing an untapped existing desire among consumers, or who satisfy new demands created in this environment of constant innovation and development.

Whether a new or existing market niche, the entrepreneur relies on others' desires to turn a profit. On one interpretation of the relationship between the entrepreneur and the market, the thrifty innovator is exploiting the need of the market. It is the term 'exploit' that so many non-capitalists object to, seeking to characterise it as a form of injustice by one man over another. This is an Orwellian interpretation by the left whose *modus operandi* is to always identify a victim, regardless of the circumstances, so that they themselves may exploit the situation to further push their collectivist cause.

Notwithstanding the intentional misrepresentation of the free enterprise system by the collectivists, the conservative understands that there is also an ethical or moral dimension to all personal conduct. That moral backbone is essential. Without it, the system corrupts and becomes fertile ground for disingenuous criticisms and misguided reforms. The business arena is no different. While capitalism does allow the individual the maximum opportunity to profit from their endeavours, it also provides scope to take advantage of others or misuse scarce resources. Where the resources in question are those residing in public ownership, the sense of responsibility for the stewardship of those gifts requires an appropriate (but limited) guiding hand. There is no universal formula that these considerations must abide by; they must be assessed and determined on a case-by-case basis as the circumstances require. The only universal code applicable here is the conservative disposition and attitude.

This is why *we need a conservative revolution.*

## Role of government

In the case of our Western democracy, that 'guiding hand' is government. Government impacts the free enterprise system in many ways. Increased bureaucratic requirements (what is often referred to as 'red tape'), direct and indirect taxation and licensing or prohibition, all of these things affect the legitimacy or potential of any given business activity.

In one sense, the government can be seen as an impediment to a true laissez-faire economy. This, however, is an ideological view which fails to recognise the benefit or value in government because of the risk of system corruption. In a way, this is the same error that contemporary socialists make when they say that the recent global financial troubles have signalled the death of the free market. The conservative considers the limited role of government within the free enterprise system as an important protector of freedom.

Limiting the government's power through decentralisation is one structural way that the corruption can be avoided. The question as to where the line is to be drawn before legitimate decentralised government becomes 'big government' is an ongoing debate between the economic libertarians and traditional conservatives. For our purposes, we will simply be guided by the principles already outlined above, which will shape policy for the following objectives:

1. to foster individual responsibility;
2. to maintain the fundamental right to personal property;
3. to ensure that all economic activity is conducted within a healthy moral framework, as described in the first half of this volume;
4. to adhere to the principle of subsidiarity at all times.

We have previously discussed the impossible ideal of unfettered freedom and its incompatibility with an orderly civil society. Simply put, this is because one person's freedom may infringe or conflict with another's. Thus under the free enterprise system, the main role of government is to codify societal expectations in the form of laws and then to enforce and uphold those laws through the appropriate institutions – namely the police and the judiciary.

Thus government has the power and obligation to maintain law and order, protect private property rights and enforce voluntary contracts between individuals and businesses.

There are other roles for government that arguably cannot or should not be fulfilled through the free enterprise system. One such area is national defence, where it would be impractical and unwise to allow any individual or business to dominate such a vital area of national interest. Indeed, even if it were at all feasible for a single, private body to operate a national defence system, the conflict between national interest and private interest would make even the prospect of a privately owned national defence body simply untenable.

Since the heart of the free enterprise system is the voluntary exchange of labour, goods and services in return for (usually) financial consideration, the government has a critical role in ensuring that contractual obligations are met in accordance with the law. Similarly, the protection of property rights is integral to the operation of free enterprise and a function best served by government in accordance with the law. American paleolibertarian Lew Rockwell notes that:

> if private property is secure, we can count on all other aspects of society to be free and prosperous. Society cannot manage itself unless its members own and control property; or, conversely, if property is in the hands of the state, it will

manage society with the catastrophic results we know so
well.[119]

Therefore the conservative accepts that private control of
property is the nerve centre of the free enterprise system with its
market-oriented price mechanism determining the allocation of
resources. The market price alone most efficiently determines the
value of one's assets and thereby encourages the most efficient use
of resources to best satisfy human needs and desires. This allows
the entrepreneur to identify, assess and pursue business opportunities
that will allow him to fulfil his objectives through the satisfaction of
his neighbours' wants and desires. Without access to secure property
rights, this important safeguard for efficiency is lost. Thus property
must be held privately and with legal security for the free market to
operate effectively.

In recent history many of the intervening acts of government
have been intended to 'protect' individuals from their own actions.
Today there are rules and regulations seemingly governing every
aspect of trade, commerce and conduct. While the motivation and
reasoning behind some of these dictates are founded on the good
intentions of the lawmaker, the result is inevitably higher product
costs and a stifled culture of entrepreneurship. Thus the consumer,
the worker and the business owner are all disadvantaged by excessive
government regulation of the free market.

The conservative understands what big government advocates
and other leftists don't: that inequality will always exist no matter

---

119 Llewellyn H. Rockwell Jr., *Speaking Liberally* (Ludwig von Mises Institute, 2003) p.
312. It should be noted however, that although it was a valid descriptor at the time
of the publication of this book, Rockwell no longer uses the prefix 'paleo' to describe
his political theories due to the confusion with paleoconservatism: Lew Rockwell inter-
viewed by Kenny Johnsson, 'Do You Consider Yourself a Libertarian?' LewRockwell.
Com (25 March 2007) <www.lewrockwell.com> (accessed 11 July 2013).

how many rules are imposed to 'level the playing field'. People have different talents and potentialities, many of which are inherited or passed down through family cultures or their particular national traditions. Likewise, human nature being what it is, unscrupulous operators will always take advantage of the naïve and criminals will still commit crimes, regardless of the legislative environment or the idealism of policy analysts and ministerial bureaucrats.

However, the failing of leftist governments is not necessarily in their failure to pursue these lawbreakers through the policing, investigative and judicial systems. Rather, leftist government fail society through their efforts to protect individuals from the consequences of their own actions. Not satisfied with an increase in regulation, government too often tries to soothe every perceived grievance through the reallocation of taxpayers' money. It is not surprising therefore that many people who do not need such government assistance see their hard-earned taxes being squandered on the unaccountable negligence of others. This does not suggest that there are not people in society who have suffered economic hardship, and sometimes through no fault of their own – a conservative who believes in the value of community will incline to believe that government may indeed have a role to play here. However, in modern Western societies, this balance of considerations has been radically disturbed by the utopian thinking of slavish 'progressive' ideologues.

Likewise, at a corporate level, bailouts and the transfer of debts from private to public ownership are justified by big government advocates as 'protecting the public' or that the enterprise was 'too big to fail'. Thus corporations are implicitly given a government guarantee to operate while the individual entrepreneur is left to profit or perish. Feelings of acrimony will naturally grow among the small business class and individual taxpayers. In their eyes, they must foot the bill for the thoughtlessness of those who appear to be shielded from their own failures. To the conservative, economic accountability is a vital check against the corruption of the free market and capitalist system. The removal of this accountability, along with over-regulation for leftist goals, largely contributed to the recent global financial troubles. As the conservative supports the principle of subsidiarity, the prudent management of business operations should apply equally to corporation and small business alike.

While all government activities will have an indirect impact on business through the economic and social environment created, as we can see there are two elements that are of critical importance to most small business owners. They are taxation and workplace relations.

### *Taxation*

The late Ronald Kitching in his book *Understanding Personal and Economic Liberty* (2005) observed that:

> until 1901, scarcely anybody paid any income tax. "We will only be taxing the rich", politicians quipped. "And in any case, tax will only be three pence in the pound (of 240 pence). Canberra will cost the average man no more per annum than a dog licence." We can now say "Some dog – Some licence".[120]

Kitching is of course correct in suggesting that taxpayers have received an increasingly poor return for their taxation burden as a means of preventing the inappropriate exploitation of public goods.

Tax freedom day is the day in which those citizens who are engaged in paid work notionally stop working to pay tax and begin to earn for themselves.

---

120 Ronald Kitching, *Understanding Personal and Economic Liberty* (CopyRight Publishing, 2005, Australian ed.) p. 23.

In 2013 tax freedom day was declared on 7 April 2013 – a full 97 days of effort before people start earning for themselves.[121] During the 1960s it was only 74 days.[122] This is a pertinent reminder of the voracious appetite for growth of the modern state.

This is again illustrated by the progression in top marginal tax rates in the last 55 years. As Kitching observed when Arthur Fadden was Treasurer (1954) the top tax rate commenced at over 17 times average weekly earnings.[123] Today it is just over two times the average wage.

In the decade to 2008, according to the Australian Bureau of Statistics, Australian taxation increased by an average of 72 per cent while the average full time weekly earnings increased by only 60 per cent.[124] This clearly accounts for the increased financial pressures facing families in Australia today.

Adam Smith set out four canons of taxation, acknowledging the need for tax as the price to pay for living in a civilised and orderly society.[125] These principles have endured the rigours of critical examination for over 200 years, yet seem to have been forgotten by modern day legislators. Smith suggested that:

1. Tax should be levied in proportion to the income received by the individual in proportion to abilities.

2. All tax requirements must be clear to the taxpayer in respect to the quantity, manner and time of their obligation.

---

121 Alexander Philipatos, 'Tax Freedom at Last', The Centre for Independent Studies (5 April 2013) <www.cis.org.au> (accessed 17 July 2013)
122 James Campbell and Laurie Nowell, '101 days' toil ... and you've paid your tax', *Sunday Herald Sun* (11 April 2010) p. 20.
123 Kitching *op cit.*, p. 33.
124 Campbell and Nowell *op cit.*, p. 20.
125 Adam Smith, *The Wealth of Nations* bk. V ch. II (Hambling and Seyfang, 1811) vol. III pp. 260-263.

3. The convenience of the taxpayer must be considered before levying taxes.

4. Taxation should be designed to take as little as possible above the demands of the public treasury.

Clearly the modern age has ignored these enduring principles in favour of a complex, bureaucratic and cumbersome system of taxation that encourages uncertainty, fosters confusion and therefore provides fertile ground for a failure in public faith resulting in tax avoidance and fraud. The fact that much of the burden of taxation collection and compliance falls upon small business has led to fewer citizens being prepared to take the risk associated with individual entrepreneurship. One does not have to be an economist to predict that this will result in a feebler economic system where innovation suffers and wealth acquisition is severely hampered. It also leads to a society where personal confidence and the spirit of enterprise will be significantly dampened. In all, it leads to a poorer and more slavish society. In other words, and as American entrepreneur Steve Forbes has commented that:

> taxes not only are a way for the government to raise revenue but are also a price and a burden. The tax you pay on income is the price you pay for working; the tax you pay on profit is the price you pay for being successful; the tax you pay on capital gains is the price you pay for taking risks that pan out. The principle is simple: If you lower the price and burden on good things, such as success, productive work and risk taking, you'll get more of them; raise the price, you'll get less.[126]

Excessive taxation or regulatory compliance also acts as a

126 Steve Forbes, 'Improving Our Lot' Forbes (online) (22 March 2007 at 6:00am) <www.forbes.com> (accessed 7 July 2013).

disincentive for many entrepreneurs. The conservative understands that allowing people to keep more of their own money is central to maintaining a limited government system that supports individual enterprise. A low tax system also acknowledges that individuals are best placed to decide how best to spend their own money and will always satisfy their personal wants and needs more efficiently than any government. That is why *we need a conservative revolution.*

### *Employment*

Similarly, the ability for individuals to negotiate working terms and conditions directly with their employers is a key catalyst to productivity and incentive.

Such a system is predicated on the enduring fact that every individual may have different priorities that will influence their ability to contribute productively to their own economic wellbeing and that of their employer and his business. It therefore offers maximum freedom of choice to both the employer and the employee.

Consider as an example, an employee with young school children. Surely such an employee should be free to negotiate an acceptable workplace agreement directly with their employer; one that provides mutual satisfaction, free from government or union interference. If the employee wants to finish at 3pm during the week and work on Sundays, and that is acceptable to the employer, why can't it be done free of penalty rates or other barriers?

Surely the freedom to determine the price and conditions of one's labour is the very basis of individual liberty in the economic sphere?

Naturally the freedom offered by such a system would, at different times within the economic cycle, provide an advantage to either the employer or employee. In a buoyant economy, where employees were in high demand, they could negotiate attractive rates of pay and other benefits in return for their labour. Conversely, during periods of economic contraction or slow growth, the employers would be able to negotiate to their own interest.

While this may seem unfair to those who seek the security of a government legislated outcome, the result is one which would maintain high levels of employment and innovation and enterprise through the business cycle. It would also ensure the survivability of many small businesses during tough economic times. Surely it is better for more people to be employed, even at a lower wage, during an economic contraction than having them languish on the welfare queues? Under such a system, the government's role would be limited to ensuring that negotiations between the parties are conducted according to agreed general principles and that the workplace itself complied with standards ensuring it was safe for the employee.

For small business, such change to employment laws would be a revolution in itself. Too many business owners are scared to increase employment levels because of the restrictive on-costs or the possibility of hiring the wrong person. On-costs are those taxes and charges that governments impose on growing businesses as they become more successful. State sanctioned duties like payroll tax act as a disincentive to employment and work against domestic industrial growth. So too do the antiquated and government mandated unfair dismissal laws that prevent a business owner from taking action without going through a painful series of steps before dismissing an employee.

In the case of an under-performing staff member, a series of warnings are required – both verbal and written – before they can be dismissed. It is not uncommon that the employee already knows the ultimate outcome and spends their 'warning' period being disruptive and unproductive. For the small business owner this can be severely damaging and even devastating to their legitimate business interests.

For example, not only do disgruntled employees create problems within the team in which they work, in a retail environment their behaviour can also directly affect trade. A staff member that is rude or belligerent to customers can devastate the reputation of a small business in a very short space of time.

Thus small businesses need to be empowered to hire and fire employees free of illegitimate government interference. Under such a system, both good employers and employees would be highly valued and therefore in high demand. This would also allow the business owner to maximise his profits and provide incentive to build a bigger and better business. This would generate greater employment opportunities and economic growth, benefiting the entire community.

For employees, the freedom to negotiate directly with their employer would allow them to prioritise their own requirements and also provide an incentive to provide maximum value for their employer.

A truly free enterprise approach to small business employment would also facilitate the employment of those with disabilities or those suffering impairment. While being motivated by the desire to treat people equally, the 'progressive' labour market reformer's policies can often produce unfair and inequitable results. This is because the leftist policy of doctrinaire equal treatment will result in treating people who are fundamentally different according to the same standards, some of which may be inappropriate or unjust, depending on each individual case. It is not reasonable to treat the disabled or impaired employee as if they were not disabled or impaired. Such an employee may have special skills elsewhere which may attract higher remuneration compared to his other peers. Likewise, if his skills and talents are limited, it is not just to demand that an employer pay him at the same commensurable rate as his peers. Justice in these situations can only be found by treating each employee as the individual that they are. Broad-sweeping policies that aim to 'level the playing field' or redress some perceived wrong do not achieve this end, they only replace one problem with another.

The conservatives' support for free enterprise is driven by their support for the dignity of the individual and recognition that enterprise is important to prosperity. These values have suffered in our society. That is why *we need a conservative revolution*.

# 6

# Freedom

A shallow definition of 'freedom' is that it is made possible simply by the satisfaction of individual desire. Such a 'freedom' is not, as we well know, afforded to everyone, nor can it ever be.

Since individuals living within a particular community will naturally develop conflicting interests, conflicting desires will need to be mediated through customs, taboos, laws and other cultural norms. Here again we are reminded of the primacy of tradition and its relevance in contemporary times.

Freedom therefore is something other than the unfettered ability to do as one pleases. Freedom must also contain within it some framework within which individuals can be free without interfering with the freedom of their neighbours. Paradoxically, profound freedom therefore necessarily requires some form of restriction. Here we are reminded of the primacy of the moral backbone without which society would be rudderless and freedom would degenerate into simple anarchy.

The opportunities that freedom provides are potentially limitless, the realities of its absence and the future for such a society can be bleak.

It is this profound form of freedom that interests the conservative. As man has no liberty while desperately surviving life in the jungle among lions, shallow anarchic freedom is rejected by the conservative who believes that human dignity is absolutely vital for the maintenance of any civilised community.

The primacy of tradition and the importance of the moral backbone have already been discussed in this volume. For a practical policy position, and put simply, the key to strengthening and maintaining freedom for a conservative government is to ensure that government's size is restricted, and that it is accountable to the people it strives to represent. Furthermore, this profound freedom is fostered through a consistent commitment to principles, and by insisting on such principles' affirmation and defence. This becomes especially incumbent on the conservative in difficult times when such principles are tried and tested.

Words such as 'freedom' and 'liberty' are heard rhetorically from many people in many situations. They are spoken so often that over time, we may cease to link them with any real meaning. The idea that "freedom is never more than one generation away from extinction"[127] should not be considered alarmist or unrealistic. We can develop effective social structures today, but without a fundamental belief in freedom and the paths to it, tomorrow holds no certainty. The only guarantee that history can give us is that a free yet complacent people will eventually have their goodwill abused by those exploiting that complacency. If any people value their freedom, properly understood, they must take active steps to safeguard it; simply enjoying it, by constant 'progressive' harping about 'rights' and demands for ever more entitlements to special interest groups, is not enough – often, it can actually be counterproductive or damaging.

So let us not be so concerned with speaking generally about freedom that we neglect to explain what it really means: freedom to

---

127 Ronald Reagan, Address to the Phoenix Chamber of Commerce (30 March 1961).

pursue one's own dreams and interests within the cultural framework which has served to protect and enrich our civilisation; freedom to build a life based on personal faith and values which reinforce and build upon a shared historical experience; freedom to make Australia an even stronger and confident nation, and in turn, the world a better place. This has been the catalyst for humanity's great leaps forward in science, art and politics, but it is not a mere abstract notion. It is a real, serious one that we risk losing unless we are prepared to reinforce it through constructive social policy and law.

Australia has paid a high price for its liberty. Those who have served our nation and sacrificed for its cause – in times of both war and peace – are among its true heroes. Thousands have given their lives so that we may benefit, and it is in their name that we must continue to protect and defend their legacy. With strength, courage and pride, we must continually reinforce our commitment to the freedom and liberty that they have earned and which we can now enjoy.

Our nation was originally founded as a penal colony after the New World severed its political ties with the British Empire. John Quick and Robert Garran wrote:

> The southern hemisphere was destined to present to Great Britain a new Colonial Empire to replace the one that was lost. The same year, during which the Americans were welded "into a more perfect union" by their federal constitution of 1787, saw Captain Arthur Phillip, with the "first fleet," on his way to the Southern Ocean in order to establish a settlement on the eastern shores of Australia, which had just been discovered and explored by Captain Cook.[128]

---

128 John Quick and Robert Garran, *The Annotated Constitution of the Australian Commonwealth* (Butterworths, 2002; originally published in 1901) p. 23.

The early colonial history of Australia was defined by a people who could not be considered 'free' in the sense we understand the word today. A significant proportion of the early inhabitants of the colony was 'in chains' while another group administered the system in an autocratic manner. Conditions then were harsh, and we should not judge the early colonists by our modern liberal standards which do not appreciate the circumstances those early settlers lived in and the world they had to deal with.

Nevertheless, it is not surprising that the uniquely Australian sense of egalitarianism would eventually be fostered in a society with such modest beginnings. After all, this was a society which would learn the value of civil and political liberty first by experiencing its absence. On one interpretation, the culture of 'fair go' is therefore quintessentially Australian. It is perhaps one reason why class-based revolutions have never found fertile ground here, and are unlikely to find mass popular support among the descendants of these early settlers or those who identify with their cultural and historical legacy. Perhaps this is why we have often been described as 'the lucky country'.

Even those who took part in the Eureka Stockade uprising (which was an infinitesimally small affair compared to other watershed events in cousin societies, such as the American Civil War) eventually managed to find a place within the political establishment of their times after the dust had settled. The culture we Australians have inherited and shaped is simply not conducive to guillotines, killing fields or gulags. Revolution is not in our spirit; we prefer other methods to resolve social disharmony and popular grievance. We have only our forefathers to thank for this; it is perhaps their greatest gift to us today.

Our nation was founded and has been shaped by these people. But it has also been shaped in recent times by those who have sought and found the freedom already established over two hundred years, without which the present society that has been built here would simply not be possible. Settlers, as well as recent migrants have all come to Australia with dreams for themselves and their families, and have displayed great determination in making these a reality. They have come with their own unique contributions to society, and where these have made us stronger as a nation, they should certainly be acknowledged as such. This is because they contribute to the cultural wealth that allows us to develop and innovate into a modern society, and also because their insights make our country a more formidable actor on the international stage. These assimilated newcomers represent part of our current social capital. We must not forget their stories, because in so many cases these can also reflect the experiences of our parents, friends and the local communities we all come from.

But while we are capable of embracing the new that can truly enrich us, we must constantly be mindful of the importance of a unified culture and the imperative to maintain it. No society can exist where its people live according to drastically differing norms and standards. Over time, such societies have been shown to polarise, fracture, and dissolve, sometimes violently. For these reasons, it is certainly not immoral to ensure that policy and law exists within a certain moral and historical framework. Just as freedom can only be truly free if it exists within a set of cultural and moral parameters, so too we cannot allow our goodwill to be abused by us being completely unquestioning and nonjudgmental in our attitudes to new ideas. Today, despite different backgrounds, those of us who are willing to respect the traditions and history of this country can join together under one national banner as Australians. This is the kind of unity that the conservative will embrace, not the superficial and divisive 'diversity' talk of the radical, who prefers to constantly re-create the nation according to some momentary fashionable utopian image and denounces all patriotic sentiment as jingoist and bigoted.

The radical shows no concern for the past, its lessons and those who created the society we can all enjoy today; the conservative looks into the future, while understanding the wealth of knowledge and insight the past has to offer. It is this *particularly conservative understanding* of unity that we must draw inspiration from when making national decisions, remembering that our shared legacy as well as our common aspirations are far more powerful than our petty differences.

To put it differently, a cohesive society relies on a balance between two apparently opposing forces: liberalism and conservatism. The tension that this causes can be resolved by finding the delicate balance between the tolerance of individual differences and respect for the choices that characterise these on one hand, and recognition of the fact that some values are better than others on the other. The genuinely conservative government will not shy away from drawing necessary distinctions between what is compatible with a free society and what is not conducive to maintaining a stable body politic. If we insist on an unquestioning equivalence of ideas, we risk dismantling the traditions of our social estate.

Likewise, on a micro level, conservative commentator Luke Torrisi instructs parents to educate their children in the rich cultural legacies that form their identity: "What stories, songs, tales, dramas even lullabies will you share with your children in order to convey to them their identity and their values?" he asks.[129] The purveyors of 'multiculturalism' often forget that a strong identity is also essential for the descendents of our settlers and those who identify with their

129 Luke Torrisi, 'Conservative Tales No. 1: The Instruction of Tradition' *SydneyTrads – Weblog of the Sydney Traditionalist Forum* (29 October 2012) <sydneytrads.com> (accessed 6 July 2013).

historical experience, so that society remains emotionally centred and develops a healthy patriotic instinct. Torrisi reminds us of this important yet neglected truth.

The ideology of the radical and the 'progressive' cannot deliver what is needed; the present system has proven itself to be a failure, and this is why *we need a conservative revolution.*

## Sacrifice

Freedom is also inextricably linked to sacrifice and compromise. In order to maximise the level of personal freedom and autonomy in our society, we must all accept that there are limits to our choices based on the need for social stability and cohesion. The enduring principle that one can do as one chooses as long as there is no harm done to others has an instinctive appeal. Yet, whilst this approach may pass the populist test, it fails to consider the potential consequences of endorsing such a laissez-faire agenda. This has already been discussed on a theoretical level earlier in this volume. Let us now consider one tangible example of social controversy, and the policies that can affect it.

One policy area where this argument is often used is in relation to the legalisation of illicit drugs. Libertarians insist that if individuals want to take illicit drugs then that is their own choice and that society would be better off if they could do so without threat of legal sanction. After all, these proponents suggest, the immediate effect of illicit drugs and the longer term consequences are borne by the individual concerned.

This suggestion ignores the *social* implications of the action of those who choose to go down this path. Firstly, we all bear the consequences of the behaviour of those under the effect of illicit drugs. This is manifested in post-use behavioural issues, the impact this has on crime, family breakdown and the social pathologies that follow and touch us all, as well as the long-term mental health implications of drug users themselves and the broader societal concerns that are a common result of systematic drug abuse.

Thus when the conservative discusses freedom, he accepts that while maximising it is a worthy goal, it must nevertheless always be balanced by the broader need for a cohesive and stable community. The notion that we should allow individuals to pursue self-destructive activities in the name of freedom sits uncomfortably with many conservatives because we see unbridled freedom as no freedom at all.

A natural evolution of this view defines the conservative attitude to community. For far too long we have heard the leftist slogan, "we live in a society, not an economy."[130] Perhaps this has gained popularity because, with the pre-eminence of economic concerns in recent decades, we have allowed materialists and economic reductionists to shape what passes for conservative discourse. The slogan is used to defame and paint us as heartless individuals whose concerns are self-centred, purely financial and material. Nothing could be further from the truth.

Conservatives accept that each of us has an obligation to offer help to those in need or caught in a spiral of self-harm. This derives from our Christian heritage and the manner in which it has shaped our politics. Here, once again we see the legitimacy of our common religious heritage and the necessary moral lessons it has imparted to us. But while the conservative acknowledges that he may have an obligation to his neighbour, he cannot force his neighbour to accept such help. Here is the influence of our Christian concept of virtue, which, as

---

130 Christine Milne, Address to the National Press Club, 'Australian Democracy at the Crossroads: the mining industry and the quarry past versus the people and the innovative future', Commonwealth Parliament House, Canberra ACT (19 February 2013).

discussed earlier, must always be voluntary to be truly virtuous. As the conservative accepts that he cannot afford *not* to extend the hand of support in some cases, that support must be accepted voluntarily by the citizen in need. This means that the 'beggar' in Adam Smith's analogy must be willing to reform if he wishes to be the recipient of the conservative government's charity. In other words, the change must come from within, not from the heights of the bureaucratic Leviathan.

Generally society should demand that individuals bear responsibility for the consequences of their own actions. Where government has sought to shield citizens from such accountability, the power and influence of government has expanded commensurately, and the autonomy or self-determination of the individual suffers as a result. An unnecessary expansion in the size or power of government is not consistent with the conservatives' ideals of limited government or maximising individual liberty.

Thus freedom brings with it responsibility – both for individuals and for the state. Individuals must accept the consequences of their actions while the state must also insist that they do so. Such an approach reaffirms the concept that the individual is sovereign, but in choosing to live within a particular nation they also agree to adhere to the laws and customs of that land as the price of living in a civilised nation. The libertarian and the radical may consider this an 'imposition of morality' on a society – the conservative considers this to be common sense.

It is easy for the beguiling lure of state assistance as a salve for every wound to be welcomed by the well-intentioned. However, every intervention by government acts to condition its citizenry to think that whatever the ailment, the cure is for the government to 'do something'.

In recent times, even notionally conservative governments have pursued a path of engorging bureaucracy as a means of responding to public pressure to be seen to respond to a problem that should properly be dealt with under the principles of subsidiarity. This has resulted in massively increased public borrowing by most Western governments: a circumstance that places an ever-increasing financial burden on taxpayers. It is a simple truth that, barring default, every dollar borrowed has to be repaid through future revenue. Thus, by demanding that government make our lives easier now, we are mortgaging the financial future of our children.

Given the opportunity, most families hope to leave a positive legacy for their descendants, so why should we expect anything less from our government?

A comment frequently attributed to Ronald Reagan, Barry Goldwater, Gerald Ford, and other United States conservative Republicans, is that "a government big enough to give you anything you want is powerful enough to take everything you have". In the 1950s, '60s and '70s, the phrase was often cited by these conservatives during their debates against big-government opponents within and without their party. At the time, the Communist bloc provided a very clear example of the threat to freedom of a collectivist government. Of course, there were (and still are) advocates for government central planning. Regrettably, many of these now reside in centre-right political parties rather than being contained in the left.

And this is one of the political challenges the conservative will have to face: the need to arrest the morphing of collectivist and freedom-destroying ideologies into mainstream political policy. Such occurrences happen when the voting public can no longer draw a distinction between the traditional political divide. When supposed conservatives argue in support of old school Marxism because it is dressed up in a green cloak to gain popular support, it is clear that conservative principles have been abandoned.

Is it any wonder then that most voters are cynical of their governments when centre-left parties are promoting themselves as 'economic conservatives' whilst nationalising industry and banks (or, for that matter, wrapping themselves in the flag and patriotic language, while promoting reforms that expose traditional communities to the socially dissolving and corrosive forces of globalisation)?

A similar conclusion can be drawn when centre-right political parties continue deficit spending through fear of making the decisions necessary to restore fiscal conservatism. It is clear the hesitancy to do so is often driven by the desire to remain in government, but it is also apparent that there is also a lack of philosophical commitment among many self-professed conservatives.

The survival instinct of our political representatives will never diminish, but history shows us that leaders who demonstrate conviction generally fare better than those without it. They are also more likely to be remembered as visionaries or reformers. Greatness lies in courage, and the politician who slavishly follows fashionable trends is rarely one who stands on principle. In turn, those that stand on principle rarely find their political work to be an easy job: it may be thankless while the task is at hand, but in the long run, maintaining a sense of integrity is a reward in itself. Public acknowledgment, if and when it comes, provides the vindication needed to turn one pioneer's work into a mission around which a following can form.

As the conservative revolution gains pace and the general public once again becomes aware of the benefits of self-reliance as well as the conservative principles outlined in this volume, they will expect accountability and responsibility from their elected representatives, just as they will demand a restoration and the safeguarding of traditional liberties and freedoms, as they are defined here. Of course, this liberty and freedom will come at a price. It will require the dismantling of the welfare state and the un-encumbering of our education system which is presently captive to orthodox leftist ideology. Thus social policy and education reform will feature prominently in the policy platform of any genuinely conservative government of the future.

The 'welfare state' promotes the notion that the individual is somehow entitled to some financial benefit from the state, without regard to their circumstance or ability to improve it. As outlined previously, the conservative is mindful and receptive to the responsibility that government may have to assist those in genuine need (such as those who are unable to work or sustain themselves for a variety of legitimate reasons), but he cannot expect working people to contribute a significant portion of their tax dollars to the poor choices or passive welfare collection of a minority.

There is also a significant change required within our educational system to ensure freedom of thought can be fostered among the future professional class of the nation. It has been well documented that our educational institutions are considered to be bastions of left activism. On its own, leftist political agitation on campus can be considered a painful birth of political awareness that, more often than not, works its way out of adolescence as the realities of life confront the young socialist. Although somewhat unkind to young conservatives, there is truth in the jibe, often misattributed to Churchill: 'Show me a young conservative and I'll show you someone with no heart. Show me an old liberal and I'll show you someone with no brains.'

However indulgent the conservative may be of the errors of youthful judgement, there can be no excuse for the institutionalised bias toward leftist dogma that exists in many of our academic institutions. Our educational bodies should be equipping our future leaders with the skills in *how* to think, not *what* to think. Unfortunately, there is growing evidence that the fifth estate has been miserably failing in its duties for some time.

The left's long march through the institutions has resulted in serious problems for academic freedom in Australia. Nigel Freitas, the Director of the 2008 Make Education Fair Campaign, collected a significant volume of documents and evidence from around Australia, which showed the ideologically oppressive and intolerant environment that conservative students face every day on campus. In his report, he submitted to the Australian Senate that:[131]

- there was a serious lack of diversity of views amongst academics;
- educators were far too willing to use the classroom to promote their political views;
- free speech was constrained on university campuses with only certain points of view deemed acceptable forms of expression;
- the insertion of extreme left viewpoints into both high school and university curricula was done with the intent to indoctrinate students with those views, accompanied by a silencing of dissenting opinions;
- a focus on 'social justice' topics by teachers, rather than on hard disciplines, has resulted in an alarming drop in both literacy and numeracy among students.

Freitas followed up those claims with a number of examples including the profiles of various academics, an analysis of the campus environment, extracts from course guides and course

---

131 Nigel Freitas, Campaign Director: Make Education Fair, Senate Submission to the Standing Committee on Education, Employment and Workplace Relations (August 2008).

descriptions, all of which exhibit a dangerous bias within the university community.

The academic profiles included an assortment of anarchists, radical feminists and socialists who are so-called 'experts' on race, whiteness, racism, religion and what they refer to as queer theory. Materials produced by one student union depicted the then Australian Prime Minister John Howard in front of a Nazi flag and suggestions that activists "plant a pipe bomb in your nearest Liberal Party office."[132]

Freitas' paper details many examples of biased and suggestive curricula and study guides that seek to further undermine our social norms in favour of a highly ideological Marxist worldview. He notes that within the major arts subjects available at the major universities, they are, almost without exception, viewed through the prism of gender, race, ethnicity, class or sexuality. These are the tools of cultural Marxism as it wages its psychological war against the traditional West in the minds of our youth.

Even within the disciplines of business or commerce, the subject of bias or tutor-directed thinking is evident. One university student taking Industrial Relations as a subject within the business stream was advised that their course marks for non-attendance at tutorials would be better if they did not attend. The student was left under no illusions that this was because they continually challenged the pro-union bias of the tutor. He ultimately received a 'B' grading without attending any further subject tutorials.

---

132 Foreign readers note: as with most Westminster systems of government, Australian politics is dominated by two major parties. The Liberal Party is popularly acknowledged as the conservative oppositional party to the Labor Party. The then Prime Minister was John Howard, who once described himself as the most conservative leader the Liberal Party has ever had. He proved to be the leftist *bete noir* while in office, and continues even today to be a figure much derided by radicals and 'progressives' alike.

Many similar anecdotes can be found from among the fraternity of conservative students who, more often than not, have had to acquiesce in order to achieve positive academic outcomes. These findings, of course, are nothing new, and they seem to be part of a universal experience in the universities of English-speaking countries. A decade before the Make Education Fair Campaign in Australia, Alan Kors and Harvey Silvergate published a volume about similar repressive trends on campuses in the United States. Kors and Silvergate make the point that this is part of the 'repressive tolerance' (which was discussed earlier in this volume) that considered it just to disenfranchise and defame views and opinions which dissent from leftist thought, and discriminate against those who do not form part of the leftist establishment.[133]

Such pressures are not limited to tertiary institutions. In many government-funded primary and secondary centres of learning, the traditional scholarly agenda of reading, writing and arithmetic has been subsumed by relative performance, historical revisionism and comparative morality.

While the teaching of Christianity is virtually forbidden within the public education system, the government funds an organisation that produces school booklets celebrating Islam's contribution to society.[134] One state government-funded student health booklet portrays boys as either homophobic bullies or victims of homophobia.[135] Primary

133 Alan Charles Kors and Harvey A. Silvergate, *The Shadow University – The Betrayal of Liberty on America's Campuses* (Free Press, 1998), specifically chapter 4 'Marcuse's Revenge'.
134 Details of the booklet are: Eeqbal Hassim and Jennet Cole-Adams, *Learning from One Another: Bringing Muslim Perspectives into Australian Schools,* National Centre for Excellence in Islamic Studies (2010). The National Centre for Excellence in Islamic Studies at the University of Melbourne has received funding from the Australian Government.
135 See discussion regarding the booklet and program run by the Sexual Health Information Networking Education (SHine SA) Inc: Senate Select Committee on Men's Health, Parliament of Australia (30 April 2009) pp. 75-77.

school children are taught about the horrors of climate change and how mankind is destroying the planet, indoctrinating them into the great green cult.[136]

The conservative does not argue that students should not be exposed to ideas that may not sit well within the traditionalist worldview. Learning about many of the things that are currently taught with zeal on campus may be a good and worthy process. However, what we are seeing is institutionalised closed-mindedness on the left, which is ironic since these were the pioneers of 'free thought' when the academics of today were the students of the '60s. They seem to have forgotten that education is not supposed to be indoctrination, and unless there is a very clear delineation between information and propaganda, our education system does our children and our nation a disservice.

Ultimately, given the imbalance so evident within much of the education system and the evident fact that any reform would have to be so colossal that it seems almost futile, it is time to expand the scope of choice for parents. Not simply a choice between private and public schooling, but a choice about what type of education they want for their children. This can be most effectively done through the provision of education vouchers that would be available for use at any licensed school in the country. Such a system would ensure that competition would facilitate the best possible education for children within the parameters of a core curriculum supplemented by additional learning that parents want for their children.

The result would be the natural evolution of a system of specialist schools which would offer a diverse array of opportunities presently unavailable. Some schools might offer multiple languages, extended

---

136 Bruce McDougall, 'Children taught climate of fear', *Herald Sun* (9 July 2011) p. 4.

physical activity, a focus on sciences or humanities. Some might be conservative religious or political schools whilst others might have a more traditional liberal focus. All of these choices would be available for parents to choose from. Those schools that didn't respond to demand would suffer declining enrolment and ultimately would be forced to adapt or close. Thus, instead of the present educational model which forces people to fit the system, the system would cater to the needs and wants of the people themselves. In the end, children would achieve better educational outcomes without an inherent 'group think' which currently dominates schools and universities nation-wide.

An additional benefit would be a long-term reduction in the cost of government-provided education expenditure per student, as more parents took an active role in the educational outcomes of their children. This would therefore result in a clear economic benefit to the state, while also reinvigorating the role that family plays in the private social sphere. The dysfunctional and counter-productive *status quo* has not served us well, and is likely to continue damaging future generations, weakening the capacity of our country's future intellectual wealth.

This is why *we need a conservative revolution*.

# 7

# Future

There is no reason to believe that pursuing change for its own sake will lead to improvements and beneficial innovation. Just because something is old or has been in use for a considerable time is no evidence of its illegitimacy or irrelevance. Indeed it could be argued that the older an existing institution is, the more successful it has been over time in surviving the ravages of history. Change for its own sake is usually argued through fast talk and symbolic action, and urged by those who believe Australia's challenges will be best managed by new approaches to old problems. Such an attitude cannot be said to be based on reason, and often shrouds irrational judgments and impulsive decisions. Those who see only the glittering shell of a politician's rhetoric may well miss the stark deficiency of their directives – the fundamental lack of planning that tends to accompany sweeping statements.

Transformation is all around us, whether it is social, technological, economic or political, and often it seems the world is moving ever faster. Each year brings decisions and developments that push our society into new circumstances, some of which may not have been foreseen by reformers. Many of these can test the way we see our nation and our place in the world.

It is, of course, vital for us to focus attention on the present, in order to continue steering Australia in what we believe to be the right direction. While we aspire to live virtuously, we must also demand the highest standards from our elected representatives: we must remember that it is not acceptable to maintain one set of values and morals for ourselves and another for our governments. As conservatives, we believe that living this virtuous life in the political context requires that our politicians maintain a connection with our past while still being focused on the future. Today, and every new day, should be seen for what it is: another opportunity to build on what we have instead of undermining the wealth we have inherited from generations past. In summary, we will achieve this by acknowledging the singular importance of our religious and cultural heritage, our historic legacies, maximising our independence and working towards the most efficient and effective ways for governance.

As this volume goes to print, the social revolution which is often symbolically seen as having commenced in the 1960s, has had over half a century to do its destructive work. Today we need to pause and consider where we find ourselves and what is to be done. We need to take stock of where we are, and to consider what the present direction means for Australia's future development as a nation. Critically, we need vision; those who can recognise this and see it through will be vital for the next decades that we and our children will face.

There are many big questions before us: questions about human dignity and what it means in the era of rapid technological experimentation, questions about society and how it is defined in the era of globalisation, the role of the individual in a centralising state, and the concept of liberty and freedom in a Western world increasingly forgetful of the principles on which these concepts have been founded. Concrete policy positions will also confront the conservative politician and voter alike: education, healthcare, infrastructure and the economy. These are all questions about the future of our society, our children and our families. The answers to these will shape Australia in decades to come. So far, it seems that only one voice has been heard in the provision of the answers to these demanding problems. Another voice is in dire need: one that clearly defines itself as an alternative to the stale and boring politics of the *status quo*.

What I want, and what I believe most Australians want, is to live in a nation that is safe, healthy and prosperous, one that stands up for itself and is regarded by both its citizens and the international community as a success, a nation worthy of the respect that is due.

This Australia is confident, and it is also necessarily conservative in that it builds on the past and values the treasure-trove of wisdom passed on to us by our forefathers through our inherited traditions. It affirms its history and heritage whenever possible, and although it is capable of critical analysis, it looks with suspicion on those who slander its history or undermine those traditions. Cultural vandals are never celebrated 'heroes' in this conservative Australia.

This Australia doesn't allow its public spending to get out of hand. It takes a considered approach to national challenges, and takes action when action is called for. It realises the consequences of economic mismanagement are dire and long-lasting, and that securing our place in global markets depends on our innovation and ability to compete at home and abroad. Bureaucratic mismanagement, incompetent fiscal planning, and mindless thievery through excessive taxation are no models of a 'charitable' or 'compassionate' government in this conservative Australia.

I believe we already know the solution to many of our greatest shared concerns. We know the solution and yet we routinely skirt around it, preferring to appease rather than act. The future I desire for Australia is in some ways bold. It requires a sustained commitment from a willing majority to work towards the objectives outlined here. But behind its audacity lies a commitment to what is fair, right and beneficial to us as individuals *and* as a community, a nation.

My vision builds on what the past has taught us, and applies these principles to the challenges of good governance for the 21st century. It centres on the timeless principles that have served society so well in the past and recognises that so much of what makes Australia great is found in the life that is routinely found on the local level, in our neighbourhoods, in our town centres and on our sporting fields. When these are thriving, when our people are optimistic, we have demonstrated that there is nothing we cannot achieve.

What Australia needs, now and always, are those who can see past empty promises and retain faith in life's most critical aspects. This includes a shared hope for a resilient and powerful nation, the reinforcement of personal initiative as a means to success, and a continued emphasis on traditional family values.

Democracy's greatest benefit is the opportunity for all citizens to contribute to national governance. However, there are forever going to be those who view politics with cynicism, claiming it attracts only those interested in self-promotion and empty promises. Given recent political history, this cynicism is understandable, but things don't have to be this way. I prefer to be an optimist. There are many politicians who have a strong and enduring commitment to the core conservative principles that represent the best future for our nation. They are not captive to the whims of pressure groups, lobbyists and other stakeholders acting outside the parameters of electoral politics. Instead they represent a balanced set of ideas, rooted in conservatism and centred on the maximisation of Australians' personal liberty and the further development of a civil society. We need more of these individuals in every aspect of community leadership: in families, on councils, in schools and in our Houses of Parliament. Their focus and commitment to our conservative values will be the catalyst for the conservative revolution to unfold.

There is a great difference between living in the past and learning from it, and for the conservative, understanding this distinction is vital. Making and changing policy on the run is clearly a recipe for disaster. Vague, simplified ideas may provide convenient fodder for the news media, but they are likely to disintegrate under careful scrutiny. Worse still are complex policies that some blindly endorse, not bothering to question how such changes would affect not only our lives, but those of the next generation.

In discussing the direction Australia has been taking under the leadership of 'progressive' and liberal governments of the past, we must remain focused on cutting through the hyperbole, resisting the urge for rash, alarmist predictions that have no real connection to reality. My interest lies in how to build upon our foundation and harness the potential which will allow all of our fellow citizens to achieve their goals. Once this has been reached, the interests of our nation will be equally served. A strong economy, well-supported small businesses and resilient international partnerships are critical to the future prosperity of this country; these are all within reach, so long as the right attitudes are shared among our political leaders on a state and federal level.

It is important to remember that what I am describing here is not some distant utopian vision. We already have all the necessary assets available to make this a reality. Our legal traditions of common law under our present constitutional arrangement are a solid bedrock on which to build. These, we already have with us. We also already have a functioning civil society with a skilled population still imbued with the cultural heritage that has created one of the most tranquil and promising nations on the planet. The task that faces the conservative of the 21st century may seem daunting, but we should never forget that we have the tools at hand. All we need is the will to use them.

The one threat to making this vision a reality is complacency. It is our common enemy, and filters through many aspects of life. It is reflected in the assumption that someone else will do a task that needs doing, that others can bear the responsibility of morally educating our children, finding us a job, bailing us out of financial difficulty. Complacency's partner is apathy. This is the mindset that tolerates bureaucratic sprawl, the endless imposition of state duties and levies and a lack of foresight and direction in areas such as infrastructure development, water management and schools.

Columnist Nico Colchester wrote of what he deemed 'comfortable uncertainty', warning that citizens who reach this state risk alienation from both the positive and negative forces at work in shaping their economic outlook.[137] In other words, when radicalism is considered normal, one's incentive to seek change is lost in a climate of passivity. It is a conservative government's role to recognise this slide, and to take all steps to restrict it.

Government should steer the nation towards the possibility of economic success not through central planning or grand schemes, but by applying the principles described above. It should never be a substitute for individuals' self-direction and persistence. Likewise, government should avoid socially balkanising policies which dissolve communities and make the maintenance of civil society impossible in the long term. They should do this through restraint and a reluctance to engage in utopian schemes of social engineering. These have been

---

137 For a brief discussion of Colchester's theory, see William Swann, *The Missing Middle – How Middle America Got Squeezed Out of the Public Debate* (Independent Imprints, 2008) p. 65.

tried many times, and we are presently seeing them fail in countries like the United Kingdom, the United States and in some Western European nations.

Ultimately, these problems can only be solved when the so called 'grass-roots' of each community starts to take responsibility for the things over which they have power and influence. Once we as individuals take care of our particular communities, in time the national question will take care of itself. Most importantly, such 'grass-root' activism will provide the important political capital for genuine conservative politicians to stand up and be counted in our Houses of Parliament. Thus, the most important way conservative voters can break their cynicism is to first vanquish the apathy that holds them back from acting where they can. Shifting our responsibilities to others may seem easy, even reasonable at first, but inevitably we will lament the loss of personal power that comes with this deferral, and ultimately desire its eventual return. Reversing this power shift is not an easy process, but it is a necessary one because without it we no longer have control over our own destinies. This must be emphasised: *there will be no shortcuts in the conservative revolution.*

Witness governments (and there have been many) who are supplied with more authority by the people who they are supposed to represent, and the inevitable consequences of such power deferral. Governments act on behalf of the electorate; their power is wielded in their name. But in a mass pluralistic society like a modern liberal democracy, there will always be a section of this electorate, sometimes a sizable one, which will feel betrayed or whose confidence will be tested. Therefore the more power and authority is deferred to a central government, the greater the frequency and magnitude of mass public disaffection. The results are a mistrustful and often downtrodden citizenry who resent their elected leaders, increasingly lamenting their influence, but who are fundamentally unable to curb or restrict it. The best way to avoid this trap is the conservative bias towards small government and the general decentralisation of all executive authority.

It is much harder to build a functioning, cohesive, civil society. It took our forefathers the better part of two centuries to do so here. Recklessness, on the other hand, is effortless. Through it, what was built over two hundred years can go to ruin in the span of just one or two generations. It only takes one poor government to undo years of Australians' hard work, and to start us again down the sorry road of enormous national debt and crippling economic pressure. The last time we witnessed this together as a nation was with the replacement of the Howard government, which gave us record savings and a 'Future Fund', with the ascension of the first Rudd government, which gave us record national debt within just one term of its electoral victory.

Still, pessimism is a draining and dispiriting force. We must be optimistic about what we can do because that is where we will find the will and strength for the restoration that this country presently needs. We must believe that Australia can overcome its challenges. The reward will certainly be great when this is achieved directly by the people, our struggles and efforts will be an investment into the future and a gift to our children. A sluggish bureaucracy, operating under utopian ideological conceits, disconnected from reality, unchecked and unaccountable – such a power is incapable of providing anything by way of a solution to the dysfunction we face today.

A new paradigm that focuses on empowering individuals and local communities, keeping them accountable for their decisions – such a paradigm will naturally foster the confidence needed for national restoration. This confidence should be encouraged at every level of governance, and particularly among local officials and parents – groups that are in a better position to know what their needs are than 'progressive' social engineers with a vision of a 'New Society' and a 'New Man'. Attempts to redefine the rules of nature have always ended in disaster and misery – it is time such experiments be done away with and communities allowed to follow their conscience according to the natural law under which they have flourished. They deserve the right to apply their own ideas and use their own judgment to the issues they're closest to. We can only know the good by allowing individuals and communities the opportunity to make mistakes and learn from them – that is where true wisdom comes from, not the abstract and fanciful notions of radical reformers who try to fit society and Man into some blueprint of their liking. I sincerely believe that if and when such a model of society is ever allowed to practically exist, society will become naturally conservative with time. Perhaps that is why the leftist ideologue is so afraid of allowing people to think for themselves. Perhaps this also feeds the insatiable hunger among the left for more and more executive power over the everyday affairs of the ordinary citizen.

The simple fact is this: not all questions are best answered by referral to a larger or apparently better-qualified body. When we determine a limited role for our federal government and stick to it, we are free to tackle everything else as we see fit. Such a model fits in with our understanding of virtue, human dignity and individual freedom. Any departure from it is a departure from these principles.

Marriage and the family are parts of the social and philosophical inheritance that we hold most dear. Our conservative instincts must always be to protect these institutions for their power to guarantee the conditions on which a good society can prosper. Doing so will satisfy the conservative traditions and ensure that the value of one of our most cherished and vital social institutions is maintained. Marriage must be continually promoted as an effective antidote to poverty, loneliness, poor health and a way to ensure children's wellbeing. The ease and speed with which so many couples divorce should be of concern, as should the rise of out-of-wedlock childbearing. These two facets of society compromise the stability of a child's earliest years, which invariably compromises social cohesion. For these reasons, the genuinely conservative government cannot compromise with or accommodate *any* changes or alterations to the idea of this institution. We have said this time and time again, and we will repeat it once more: *marriage is defined as a union of one man and one woman.* Anything that does not fit this definition is not a marriage at all, but an entirely different concept which has no legitimacy under natural law. Treating any such concept as if it were a marriage (by providing it with similar rights and privileges and ascribing to it the same moral standing as a marriage) is not in accordance with natural law. Accordingly, it will have potentially damaging long-term consequences for society. This is not 'bigotry' or 'intolerance', it is simple common sense.

The free market is the backbone of Australian prosperity, and a fundamental part of our economy. The ideas underpinning the free market derive from our inherited cultural legacy and religious traditions. They are also based on the understanding that what is right for one person may not be so for another. Our legacies and traditions therefore provide a system whereby different objectives and desires are mediated between individuals living together in one society. To this end, the free enterprise system provides individuals with choice. This choice, which is experienced within a framework of popularly accepted norms and standards, is the basis of a free society. Solutions to problems and obstacles can therefore be found through open competition within a market which is itself the product of a moral and culturally united society. Such a model offers liberty and freedom without exposing the individual to the corrosive effects of anarchy and social dissolution.

Thus, when conservatives talk of 'change', it is the change that stems from facilitating this kind of opportunity and freedom. It is the difference between reform and revolution. This evolutionary and reflective change is far superior in meeting popular needs that the wild experiments of social engineers or government administered service provision. This is so for the simple reason that it allows the people to direct their own lives themselves. This is not a heartless proposition, far from it; it is an important distinction to make, for we don't want a society where thousands of people resent having to support their fellow citizens. Such a society breeds suspicion and envy and is not conducive to maintaining a healthy sense of peoplehood and community.

On a practical level, the conservative acknowledges that taxes already take a sizable portion of everyday Australians' earnings. As our population ages, each tax dollar will be forced to go further. This ultimately means even important or essential services are not likely to be fully supported in the future. The answer to this is not to tax more, but to fundamentally reform government's belief in its role as wealth re-distributor so that citizens' money is not circulated through state bureaucracies before finding its way back to the people, rather that the money never leaves the citizens' pocket to begin with.

Few are happy to be part of a nation that is heading in the wrong direction, steered by bureaucrats who are too far from the people to gauge policies' effects. But unless we stand up and insist on restricting government's size, there is no reason to expect our country to work efficiently and fairly.

It's time to face the future, and it is time for conservative principles (and actions) to be applied in our personal lives and in government. The conservatism I have described in this volume will help to create the conditions in which all citizens can improve their lives and aid in improving the lives of those around them. Within the framework of this conservatism, individuals know what is best for them and what is in their best interest of their communities. We need to reaffirm the values that will create a better Australia so that all Australians have the opportunity to make the most of their talents, skills and assets.

That is what the conservative revolution is about: the application of timeless principles into the present, and looking to the future with confidence and courage. It is government's responsibility to acknowledge this as we move further into the 21st century, leaving behind the debris of the bankrupt revolutionary and 'progressive' ideologies of the past, ideologies that have caused so much misery and destruction in the last hundred years. The leftist experiment has had sufficient opportunity to prove itself, and it has failed. It is time to return to the tried and true. By embracing and trusting in the strength of the Australian people – and by empowering those who are doing the best they can, I believe that this conservative vision will serve our nation best as Australia continues to grow as a proud member of our Western Civilisation.

This is why *we need a conservative revolution.*

## What is to be done?

What are the practical steps that the individual can take to contribute to the conservative revolution and help with national restoration? The following are some ideas that can break the spirit of apathy and alienation that often seems to be plaguing society. Most of them may not be explicitly political, but that is only because they focus on rediscovering 'the good' in life, and this is a cultural exercise. I believe that right politics will naturally flow from a society which is healthy on a spiritual, cultural and emotional level.

1. **The first thing:** Realise that you have more control and impact on the people and things that are closest to you. Our own personal lives, our relationships with family and friends, and our participation within the community – these things are immediately within reach. If we are concerned with the state of our civilisation, we should, like true local patriots, 'think globally and act locally'. This too is an inherently conservative slogan which has been hijacked by the left. It's time to take it back.

2. **On the personal level:** Conduct yourself according to the principles that have been briefly discussed in the foregoing pages. Be honest and sincere in your dealings with others. Seek self-reliance so that you are never a burden to others but an asset to your community. To achieve this, strive to refine whatever talent you have. Better yourself, either through further education or vocational training, or simply by doing what you do best while striving to do it better. Work hard, render unto Caesar what is his. Do not spend more than you have. Invest in your family's and your community's future (more on this below). Reflect on your place in this world: render unto God what is His. Be actively involved in the traditions that define the culture you are part of.

3. **On the level of your family and friends:** These are your most immediate contacts with society and the nation. You are as much a part of them as they are a part of you.

   Becoming a parent is a tremendous sacrifice and joy. If you are a parent, remember your traditions and cultural heritage and ensure that this is passed onto your children. Get involved in their lives. Do not defer your responsibilities to popular media and fashionable trends – they are motivated by the drive for profit and influence and do not have your, or your children's, best interests at heart.

If you are a young Australian, acknowledge the role your parents have played in your life so that they do not feel their efforts have been in vain. In an era of family dissolution, let us take conscious steps to bring families together.

We live in troubled times, and it may be the case that you may not have any close family structures in your life. In that situation, if you want to establish a family for yourself, strive to be the parent you would want to have had. Make sure that what you pass on to your children is a positive legacy.

If this is not the situation you find yourself in, do not worry, you are still part of a community and you still have intrinsic value which can enrich it.

4. **On the level of community:** Community predates the state and its governments; without it, any sense of *belonging* will be severely impoverished. Your community will define who and what you are as much as your free choices in life.

Community is like a garden, it is an organic living thing; if it is neglected, it can overgrow with weeds and suffer decline. Communities must therefore be actively maintained.

Be involved with your local public associations, whether they are religious, sporting, social or political. All this activity is the lifeblood of culture, and this is where the essence of patriotic spirit and a sense of togetherness is born.

5. **Stay active:** Do not waste time. The pace of contemporary life however can cause alienation, so it is important that you are not unhealthily caught up in your daily work routines.

We work to live, we do not live to work.

For example, you may want to pursue a hobby which is different from your employed work. This can also include the involvement of family and friends. It could even involve some community-oriented activity.

Do not lose connection with the world around you. In a time where much of what defines our economy seems to be ethereal or intangible, including some hands-on activity in your life can help give you perspective and emotional or psychological centredness. This may not be a problem if your job already involves manual labour. Either way, doing something tangible, something 'real' can anchor a person in what is immediate and important in life. This may be particularly relevant for young men, whose traditional culture has suffered by decades of radical social engineering. Fight back by reconnecting with your nature: build something.

Staying active also means you should have time to sit back and reflect: read a book, explore the local environment, start a club. Basically: get involved.

6. **Cultural involvement:** There are different ways that you can impact the culture.

The first is to build on what already exists: take active part in the rituals and ceremonies which celebrate who and what we are as a people. On a personal level, these include the dates and milestones celebrated by family and friends. On a national level, these are times where we remember the things that define us as a nation. The most obvious would be Christmas and Easter, Australia Day, ANZAC Day, the Queen's Birthday and others. Each state in our Commonwealth may have specific local dates on which important historic events are celebrated too. Most

Australians already take part in these celebrations with enthusiasm, but it is always tempting to get caught up in the trivialities of the event and forget the substance of what is actually being remembered and how it is important today. Generally, the left has little time for these dates for a reason: they provide an important anchor for our identity, and it is always more difficult for authoritarian forces to subjugate a proud people.

The second way you can impact the culture as a conservative is to become part of a movement which seeks to foster conservative ideas among those closest to you. Start a local conservative group. Anybody can do this, and it doesn't involve having to join a political party or stand in elections (more on this below). Host regular meetings; invite your friends and family; watch a film or documentary; share some reading material, and then discuss it. Start a website and write for it if you feel your views are not getting air-time in the mainstream press. The internet is a tremendous tool for grass-roots activism, but *it should not be a substitute for real activity.* Get involved in the local community under the banner of your conservative group: *be seen.* Bring more people into the fold; network with other groups that have already been established; help each other organise. Remember the first point above: you have the most power and influence over your immediate surroundings. This does not mean being isolationist and ignorant of your compatriots elsewhere – we are all part of the same struggle for national renovation. Where possible, we should all lend each other a helping hand.

7. **Political involvement:** I have left this near the end, which may be odd for a politician, but this is by no means an oversight or afterthought. The simple fact is that the

conservative revolution that I have been calling for in these pages will naturally take care of itself if the above points are taken to heart by the citizenry.

Political involvement is not for everyone. Some people thrive in this environment, others are repelled by it. There is nothing wrong with either group. People have different talents, interests and capabilities. The conservative revolution will not succeed without the activities of all sorts of political activists. *You are all needed in the struggle ahead.*

**Voting:** In any case, *we can't afford to be ignorant of political issues.* In Australia we have compulsory voting. This means that the conservative citizen should do all things necessary to avoid being negligent at the polling booth. Unfortunately, many aspects of the conservative revolution will be opposed by forces that exist in all major parties; it is not enough simply to vote tribally. The cultural restorationist will take the time to *find out who his candidates are, and what they actually stand for.* The conservative culture warrior will be a person of substance and should vote accordingly.

**Party involvement:** Joining a political party is a good option for conservatives. If they do, while they may find themselves caught up in the shenanigans of party life, they will have an ability to contribute towards determining party candidates for elections and broader policy debates. However, making the conservative revolution a reality may be stifled at every turn by seemingly trivial distractions. This is why I believe that all serious political steps towards the conservative revolution are fundamentally *cultural.* Be that as it may, active involvement in a political party can be useful as a training ground for organisation and involvement in whatever level you feel is right for you;

becoming a member of a party can be an educational experience that will benefit the conservative revolution we're all working towards in our own individual ways.

8. **Have the right attitude:** The last and perhaps the most important point, it is absolutely essential that you *never apologise or let yourself feel guilty about your views and beliefs, never allow terms like 'conservative' to be used as a pejorative in your presence, never cower when your culture and opinions are attacked or slandered, never water-down your thoughts or views just because you think you will be shouted down by others, always stand up for what you believe courageously and with confidence, go on the offensive in debates, identify leftist hypocrisy, inconsistency and irrationality and never give it a pass.*

Many conservatives tell me that they often feel they are alone. The conservative group you join or start will help you discover that that there is a body of opinion in the community which is dissatisfied with the group-think of the left. *You are not alone.* Together, you can reinforce each other's confidence and help build the courage within to be the culture warriors that are needed to fight for a brighter future for this country.

If you do all the that you can to better yourself personally, maintain involvement with your local community, become a role model for those in your social group, stay active and engage in some form of cultural or political involvement, you will be well on the way to becoming the weapon that is needed for the conservative revolution.

These things are not difficult; they are all within an arm's reach away.

The choice is essentially yours to make.

So make it well.

# Our Australia

A nation bound by virtues and sustained by faith —
where values that reflect our moral foundation are accepted as
critical to our future.

A place where we recognise that what
is best for our families is best for society;
where children are encouraged to believe in their dreams,
and can work hard to make them real.

Let our country be one where government is not an obstacle,
but an advocate and ally of its people;
for when freedom resides with responsibility,
Australia will always prosper.

A land where determination will never succumb to apathy,
where those who receive will also give, because there is strength
in community.

We know that sustaining freedom will not be easy;
for there will always be some who seek to oppose and restrict it.

But our nation is not for those seeking an easy path,
it is for those who dream not only of today, but of what
tomorrow can be.